Introduction to
Online Journalism

Introduction to Online Journalism

Publishing News and Information

Roland De Wolk
San Francisco State University

Allyn and Bacon
Boston   London   Toronto   Sydney   Tokyo   Singapore

Series Editor: Karon Bowers
Editorial Assistant: Jennifer Becker
Marketing Manager: Jackie Aaron
Production Editor: Christopher H. Rawlings
Editorial-Production Service: Omegatype Typography, Inc.
Composition and Prepress Buyer: Linda Cox
Manufacturing Buyer: Megan Cochran
Cover Administrator: Kristina Mose-Libon
Electronic Composition: Omegatype Typography, Inc.

Between the time Web site information is gathered and then published, it is not unusual for some sites to have closed. Also, the transcription of URLs can result in unintended typographical errors. The publisher would appreciate notification where these occur so that they may be corrected in subsequent editions. Thank you.

Many of the designations used by manufacturers and sellers to distinguish their products are claimed as trademarks. Where those designations appear in this book, and Allyn and Bacon was aware of a trademark claim, the designations have been printed with an initial capital. Designations within quotation marks represent hypothetical products.

Library of Congress Cataloging-in-Publication Data

De Wolk, Roland
    Introduction to online journalism : publishing news and information / by Roland De Wolk.
      p. cm.
    Includes index.
    ISBN 0-205-28689-5 (alk. paper)
    1. Electronic journals.   I. Title.
PN4833 .D49 2001
025.06'0704–dc21

                                                     00-044209

Printed in the United States of America

10 9 8 7 6 5 4 3 2 1   05 04 03 02 01 00

For Dr. B. Edwin Blaisdell, who taught me through his long and powerful example that scholarship, honesty and true dedication are all part of the same mission: a successful life. Mine has been immeasurably better because of his.

Contents

■ chapter 3

Way New Journalism Meets Lord Northcliff   45

■ chapter 4

Gathering Digital Data   69

■ chapter **10**

Issues in the Future of Journalism   169

Preface

There is no real dispute. The combined power of pictures, graphics, audio, text and interactivity available to millions of people online is the most significant change in mass communication since television. Combining these media is the essential definition of multimedia. To have this power on the Internet in the form of the World Wide Web creates opportunities—and dangers—past our reckoning. There are credible people who argue that the Web is the most potentially powerful communications development since the invention of movable type. That remains to be seen. But if proven so, few who understand what is happening here will be surprised.

This power in its beginning stages often has been the province of the entertainment and retail industries, with real reporters desperately trying to catch up and publish online newspapers, magazines, Internet radio shows and even videos. They are increasingly, but somewhat slowly, finding success a struggle compared with the experience of sites that offer fun, distraction and, most disturbing of all, material masquerading as journalism.

Like all forces, this one engenders equal and opposite reactions. The great power of the World Wide Web does indeed make everyone a potential reporter, editor, producer and publisher. But does every person who aspires to be a journalist have the skill, the craft and the discipline to carry this power with equal responsibility? "Who is a journalist?" asks Ted Gup, who teaches journalism at Georgetown University. "Call me old-fashioned, but I believe that there is more to being a journalist than simply being heard. A thousand people may take up the microphone in karaoke, and yet not one of them may be a singer."

True students of the ancient—and modern—craft of journalism must take their rightful places and provide quality alternatives to the hustlers and the posers currently populating the Web.

The challenges are unique and historic. Quite simply, this is a new medium, and the old models atrophying in their limited forms cannot really be used in true multimedia. Historically, each new medium has been made of the same stuff as its predecessor. For example, the first movies were little more than filmed stage plays; the first radio news was mostly a promotion for newspapers and consisted of reading print stories over the air; the original television programs were basically transferred radio shows.

This pattern holds for modern journalism as well, from the expensive failure of teletext to many of today's online newspapers, which offer little more than reprints of the daily paper. Truly fresh, unencumbered approaches may be found by looking to the best colleges and universities, where students and forward-thinking professors are not stained with the soiled imprimatur of a flailing newsroom. At the same time, the now traditional, but hard-won and hard-kept, standards of good journalism should be used as a foundation on which to build a solid new world of news and information.

First-class journalism, broadcast and communication schools inveigh against sloppy reporting, editing and producing and try to instill in their students the need for accuracy, balance and fairness. These standards, so important to the profession, must be carried into the new medium as well. Telling accurate, fair and thorough stories in the ages to come must take place on the mass medium of the future: the World Wide Web segment of the Internet.

Building on those broad charges, the first comprehensive online journalism production course in the United States was developed at San Francisco State University. The first version of NewsPort (http://NewsPort.sfsu.edu) was launched in May 1996 and has kept advancing online since.

The university had some natural advantages in developing this program. First, it is located in San Francisco, truly the heart of the new information order. People from Silicon Valley to the south, and Multimedia Gulch, a few miles to the north of campus, knew about the university's journalism department and agreed to help. Second, early on, there were more Web servers and online users per capita in the San Francisco Bay area than anywhere else in the United States providing a working exposure to multimedia. Finally, the student body at San Francisco State was as diverse in interests and goals and ethnicity as could be found anywhere. They were open-minded and, most important, driven to become the journalists of the 21st century.

Some generous support, both financial and intellectual, enabled this ambitious experiment to be launched. It has been fortunate in its successes. In this volume and on the accompanying Web site are the results and lessons of the prototype.

This text provides you with a chart, a map if you will, on how to get started, to avoid traps, to overcome high-tech anxieties and to capitalize on successes. The aim is to share hard-won knowledge as newspeople do, not as computer experts. Instructors and students will find practical, useful materials in the text's companion Web site (www.abacon.com/dewolk).

This is very much an evolutionary adventure, one that will appeal to the open-minded, the exploratory, the truly fascinated about their world— in short, those with a genuine journalistic spirit.

This guide is very much an inclusive set of materials about journalism, not just a specialty book about one aspect of the future of the craft, the calling, the mission of journalism to serve as the central nervous system for human societies. It is a survey for our present and future, taking our hard-won lessons of the past into the 21st century. It is specifically designed for students and teachers of news and information, whether they are in journalism, broadcast or communications schools, or related curricula. But it is also very much for the self-taught, the distance learners, and the professionally—or personally—curious. A love of journalism and a commitment to its future are all that are required.

The result will be thousands of new writers, reporters, editors, producers and publishers online who can honestly call themselves journalists, bringing accuracy, attribution, thoroughness, fairness and compassion to the newsrooms of this new century.

■ Acknowledgments

If I have been able to peek a bit over the top of today's journalism landscape and into a bit of tomorrow's, it's because several key people helped hoist me aloft. Dr. Leonard Sellers, a partner, an inspiration and a friend comes to mind first. His keen insight, quick intelligence and fierce honesty have kept me reaching for my best and guarded me against those who would have encouraged less of me.

Gary Barker and Jesse Garnier arrive in the same thought. If there are two smarter, more able, harder working online journalists, they aren't on this planet. Their expertise, energy, thoughtfulness and artistry inspire me regularly. Their dependability, patience and attention to detail are incomparable. Gary Barker's edit of the manuscript was a crucial step in completing the work. I only wish I had paid more attention to his suggestions.

I am indebted to the following reviewers: William Tate Chronister, Kent State University; Steven Doig, Arizona State University; Jamie Murphy, Florida State University; John Pavlik, Columbia University; and Carl Sessions Stepp, University of Maryland. They made substantial, thoughtful and informed suggestions for the manuscript that speak of their grasp of scholarship, the online environment and that all-important third rail powering this entire enterprise: journalism.

The 10 guest authors featured throughout this text already have added, through their well-known work, great honor to the weighty future of journalism. I am humbled by their company.

I am indebted to the journalism department at San Francisco State University, especially to Professor Erna Smith, department chair. She stands out in academia for her relentless and passionate stand for the students. Professor Austin Long-Scott has unselfishly shared his considerable brains, wonderful sense of humor and heavily taxed time with me for longer than I deserve. If not for him, I would have missed many of the opportunities I have enjoyed. Professor John Burks has been a cheerful, bright partner and friend. Dean Nancy McDermid allowed me to go ahead with creating our online journalism experiment when most people still thought going online meant getting hung out to dry.

A special word for Richard Gingras, who started as a mentor and has become a great friend. His sharp eyes and mind, coupled with an enviable generosity of the spirit, were key to getting started and staying on course, online and off.

It would be selfish, stupid and unseemly if I did not thank my many students who have challenged my thinking, assumptions and notions about the future of journalism. I will watch with deep satisfaction as you take over an industry in need of your online journalism skills—and more important, of your integrity, compassion and dedication.

Most of all, none of this would have been possible without the single best real reporter I have ever worked with: Carla Marinucci of the San Francisco Chronicle. She coincidentally happens to be the best human being, mother of two awesome boys and wife of all time. Why she ever married me is a constant source of bafflement to everyone, including me.

About the Author

Photo by Steele Douglas.

Roland De Wolk teaches at San Francisco State University's journalism department, where he created the first original online journalism production course in the nation.

He has also taught newswriting, reporting, depth reporting and History of Journalism.

Roland De Wolk was a newspaper reporter for 15 years, has been published in newspapers and magazines around the world, is the author of two other books, and is now a television news producer in charge of in-depth and investigative reports.

He is a member of the New Media Executive Roundtable, established by the Society of Professional Journalists; is a member of Investigative Reporters and Editors; was an inaugural fellow for the Freedom Forum's New Media Technologies program; and has been the recipient of many regional, state and national journalism awards.

Roland De Wolk is a graduate of the University of California at Berkeley and grew up in the San Francisco Bay Area, where he still lives. He has traveled extensively throughout Africa, Western and Eastern Europe, the Middle East, South America and Australia.

He is married and has two sons.

Any critiques, comments or suggestions for "Introduction to Online Journalism" are enthusiastically welcomed. Please address them to the author, care of the publisher, or e-mail to rolando@sfsu.edu

Introduction

Newspapers are ancient instruments. It is easy for people, especially Americans of college age, to dismiss them because of their longevity. As with other longstanding institutions, such as the traditional religions, many loud voices claim newspapers have outlived their usefulness and must atone for their sins.

But let us turn that perspective upside down for a moment. Why do some institutions last hundreds of years? Is it in part because they answer a deep, wide and constant need of the human spirit? One needn't be a cultural anthropologist to know the answer.

Newspapers can be traced back at least to Roman times, when Acta Diurna ("Daily Acts") circulated in the Forum. It was the massive technological breakthrough of movable type in 1455 that gave newspapers a chance to live and become the force that it is today. Finally, with the vision and persistence of pioneers such as James Gordon Bennett and his

James Gordon Bennett created the New York Herald in the 1830s, effectively creating the first mass news media by his sustained effort to make news and information interesting and important to a wide audience.

The Gutenberg press remains the single biggest technological advance in the history of news and information. The technological advance took the power of writing out of the hands of a few and put it in the hands of many—a parallel not unlike the creation of the World Wide Web.

one-penny New York Herald, the mass media emerged more than 150 years ago. The potent mix of technology and capitalism created a need for news and information that continues to grow in importance to this day.

The technological advances of the Industrial Age had a huge effect on communications in general and on journalism in particular. Power presses, the telegraph, photography, radio and television have transformed the world. Mass media have been likened to the central nervous system of economies, governments and cultures.

Now an entirely new nervous system is being built, the metaphor more electrical than ever, axons and dendrites being replaced with servers and modems. The content is both traditional and new, combining the ancient need of telling stories reliably and well with the modern ability to tell them with flash, flexibility and instant international access.

The news medium now being created has the capacity for permanent storage—and instant universal retrieval. What you write today may be instantly read almost anywhere worldwide and used many, many years from now. That alone should give journalists added pause to be sure that what they are producing meets a very high standard indeed.

The potential consequences of this new medium are so great few have had a chance to study the possibilities—and dangers—it may bring. The future of journalism was the subject of a wide-ranging issue of the Media Studies Journal, published by the Media Studies Center of the Freedom Forum. Scholars and practitioners from many media looked ahead at their own areas, but one thought emerged uniting all: "There is no getting around the fact that if one trend defines the future of all media," the editors wrote, "it is their interaction with the computer and the Internet." There is also certainty in knowing that the lessons learned from centuries of evolving journalism must not be forgotten in the rush to master the technology nor be ignored by those anticipating great wealth in the news and information industries.

It can all be so daunting. Browsing through a computer magazine or listening to a salesperson droning on about RAM and bauds and pixels is enough to send many people back to TV—or even to the newspaper.

But change is here and will continue whether we participate or not. If journalists are not able to bring discipline and professionalism to the new news channels, there may come a time when even Matt Drudge will be remembered as relatively reliable.

Many promises are made to demystify going online and actually creating multimedia. This book will keep those promises, explaining, as good storytellers must, in understandable terms, what could easily be confusing. There are technical terms and (too much) jargon that comes with any discussion of computers and software and cyberspace. Although some of this terminology may be obfuscation, many of the terms have become a part of the required shorthand that comes with any discipline. At the back of the book you'll find a comprehensive glossary for whenever you hit a word or phrase that raises a question.

Words from the glossary will often be in **boldface** in the text, highlighted like some **hyperlinks** on the **World Wide Web.** It's easy to present some vital information about a **Web server,** for example, but not everyone

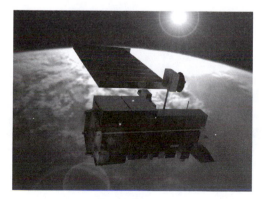

Satellites, first launched in the 1960s, allowed news and information enterprises to broadcast around the world in seconds, changing the face of communications forever.

Image by Barbara Summey, NASA GSFC.

knows what a Web server is. The glossary will explain in ways you will be able to understand.

By the same token, nothing is taken for granted about the reader's knowledge of the field of journalism—print or broadcast. Such terms as **multiple sourcing** or **B-Roll** are also in the glossary.

This book offers a mix of journalism with the latest communications technology. As with a strong epoxy or alloy, this mix will create a bond enormously powerful and flexible. It will be one that will not only make the important work of journalism available to many, but will bring the power of reliable, interesting news and information to millions seeking power over their own lives.

chapter **1**

Setting Up

This telephone has too many shortcomings to be
seriously considered as a means of communication.
The device is inherently of no value to us.
—Western Union internal memo, 1876

All good writers know that the secret ingredient in creating a great story is to stop before hitting the keyboard and to think hard about the *point* of the story. Great storytellers will start with a clear knowledge of what needs to be said, what digresses from the point and what they hope to leave with the reader long after they part company. This book begins with some sharply focused concepts on the major points of online journalism and details what it intends to accomplish.

Before journalists can begin to use and produce online journalism, they must have the tools for doing so. Because computers and computer programs can easily intimidate people, this chapter demystifies the essential first steps in deciding what journalists need on their tool bench in order to craft their work.

Online journalism, rather simply, is quality news and information posted on the Internet—especially the World Wide Web portion—where people can read, see and hear it through their computers and other similar devices. Most online journalism belongs to newspapers with online sites. Some are as high quality as their print parents (http://www.nytimes.com); some are not. Almost none take advantage of the tremendous potential for top-shelf reporting and storytelling created by the Web.

Creating high-quality online journalism is no easy task. New, previously unimagined tar pits await us, while at the same time glittering new opportunities beckon. This book will explore both. Today's online journalism represents simple baby steps. Today's journalism students will be the first generation of journalists to take this nascent power to a full run. This book will explore that path as well.

Journalists must stop and assess what they have to work with. If the telephone seemed like an odd and intimidating new tool to journalists at the beginning of the 20th century, how are we to regard the millennium we enter, which requires journalists to have familiarity with pixels, 16-bit sound and SCSI ports?

How did things get so complicated? That was, no doubt, the first question of stone cutters when they started learning how to use the new technology of knife-sharp reeds to write in moist clay and of calligraphers challenged by 290 separate characters to be set in a Gutenberg printing press. Would you like people who don't know a fact from a rumor to take the helm of news and information simply because they don't mind spending a little time learning a new technology for the World Wide Web?

No journalist would.

■ Uploading the Future

Ancient history of the World Wide Web starts in 1969. A network of computers beginning with a link between two major California universities (UCLA and Stanford) began to grow to help academic and military researchers share their raw data with one another. This is now known as the **Internet.** In March 1989, Tim Berners-Lee, a British citizen working in Switzerland, proposed a computer protocol that would allow people to send images, such as photos and graphics, on this network also. In December of 1990 that part of the Internet, the World Wide Web, went up.

In 1993 some unencumbered minds at the University of Illinois at Urbana-Champaign developed an elegant, easy-to-use and quickly popular way for people without advanced computer skills to communicate with one another on this network using words, **embedded images** and later, other media. It was called a **browser.** Although most certainly not the first, this browser was among the best—and the most marketable. In 1993, this browser, called Mosaic, began to spread beyond computer science departments into colleges of humanities and creative arts—and then to the business world. It soon evolved into Netscape (although Mosaic itself stayed around for a few years afterward) and turned into the Web's first major commercial product.

By 1994, many forward-thinking folks in mass media were talking about the Web, getting their first clever e-mail addresses (later exchanging them for simple, easy-to-remember ones), and sending **URL**s to each other.

Magazines enjoyed the first early success with breaking out of their traditional paper form, chiefly because of their better backgrounds in visual information. Those working in the magazine industry were among the first to envision the Web as an electronic version of slick, glossy print pages. "By the late 1990s, it was clear that much of the innovation in these 'new media' areas would be led by magazine firms," observes David Abrahamson, associate professor at Northwestern University's Medill School of Journalism. "In the main, the reason for this has been the fortuitous convergence between the strengths (and needs) of the magazine industry and the emerging directions in which the Web seems to be evolving." One of those key factors, Abrahamson says, is "the growing number of women online."

But there is no denying now that many in the magazine industry have since been hitting a wall, uncertain how to fully brew images, words, sound and interactivity, perhaps because magazine publishers and editors are also trapped by their training in the static world of print.

Television news executives, on the other hand, have no such excuse. Ironically, this is the reason they may have the most to lose by being the least responsive to the Web (although farsighted members of that industry see salvation in a concept discussed in depth in Chapter 6). "You can mourn if you want the end of our idea of a 'broadcast'—a place where the entire country can sit down together and get information," says Kyle Pope of the Wall Street Journal. "The dinner hour is over."

Although TV may be the furthest behind today, it most certainly has the most to lose—or gain—as the Web matures and supplants it. Consider this: the computer screen (or monitor, as it is often called) is more or less the same as the TV screen, and as digital technologies overtake the broadcast industry in the next several years, the screens will be even more

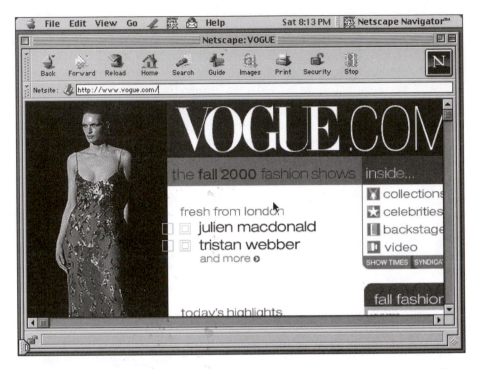

Magazines, such as Vogue, were among the first of the traditional, or old, media to understand and embrace the Web. Their attention to visual information enabled them to tap into the early potential for storytelling online.

similar. The mouse accomplishes the same function as the remote control. When these and other aspects of the two media merge, there will be no reason for viewers to turn to traditional television. They will be able to watch TV on their own terms, including, almost certainly, the ability to step away from the set for a short or prolonged period of time and not miss a second of whatever they were watching. (Already several relatively effortless digital recording devices are on the market that anticipate this development.) Viewers will be able to open an almost unlimited number of **windows** on the screen in search of more or different news, information and entertainment. In addition, there is the fabled but still somewhat murky ability to interact with various aspects of television programs.

Radio's prospects in emerging online mass media are strong, if radical. "The Internet has provided a medium for the transmission of sound files so robust, potent and flexible as to make the entire system of radio that we now take for granted into something so completely different as to be revolutionary," write Peggy Miles, of Intervox Communications and media researcher Kenneth R. Donow. "Listeners will be able to hear instantly any program from anywhere in the world." After a rather slow start, Web radio is now catching up with this predicted future, with fast-growing numbers of people listening to stations from around the world online. The next big step will be Web radio in the automobile, via satellite signals.

Newspapers were the first in the journalism community to see a threat from the World Wide Web. The newspaper industry had been challenged—and damaged—so many times in the past 100 years, it was quick to recognize a new potential predator. The (rightfully) paranoid newspaper

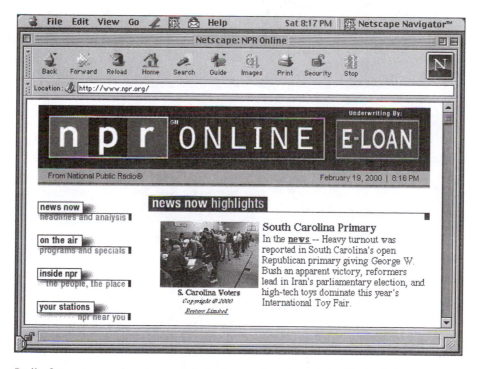

Radio faces many advantages and challenges because of the birth of the Internet. Farsighted networks such as National Public Radio have been among the first to put ambitious sites online, hoping to be among the first to stake a claim on the radio of the future.

Newspapers coast-to-coast are throwing up online news sites tend to have similar layout and news. Most are having significant trouble breaking away from their print sensibilities. The next generation of Web journalists will have to break free of these strictures to succeed.

Seattle Times Web page used with the permission of the Seattle Times Company. Copyright © 2000 by the Seattle Times Company. Detroit News Web page reprinted with permission from the Detroit News. Approved by Mark Silverman, Publisher and Editor.

companies quickly threw up sites on the Web beginning in the mid-1990s. But they took the same approach newspapers took in establishing radio stations in the early 20th century—these sites are almost always simple online versions of the print product. Words and graphics are pretty much all you'll see from newspapers online, and each one looks pretty much the same as the next.

Mario R. Garcia, a well-known newspaper and Web site designer, points out that about 85 percent of a newspaper's appearance is, in fact, type. This age-old design has transferred to most online news sites run by newspapers, despite the tremendous new possibilities opened by this entirely new medium. This point is not lost on rivals for the people seeking

news and information on the Web. Garcia wisely states that "readers are interested in information, which is not to say they are interested in news." It is the job of the journalist to create an interest in news.

Why, then, are journalists still going about using the Web the wrong way? Perhaps one of the answers lies in an examination by writer Matt Welch, in the Online Journalism Review (http://ojr.usc.edu). Welch's story points out a "blandness" among online news sites, caused in large measure by a lack of original, creative storytelling and an overreliance on Associated Press stories, churned out like sausages from a sausage factory for print, broadcast and now online outlets.

"I look around and they're all the same kind of design format, editorial content," says Salon (http://www.salon.com) founder and editor David Talbot. He and other forward-thinking journalists have made similar observations for some time. "I can't get a feel from any place I stay from reading the papers," agrees journalist Doug Thompson of Capitol Hill Blue (http://www.capitolhillblue.com/). "And if I try to get an advance feel by reading their Web sites, it's even worse."

"There's a new generation out there," concludes journalist and Web site designer G. L. Marshall, "that would readily accept a new way of handling news, and they're not being served."

Many managers in the newspaper industry are having trouble understanding why people aren't visiting their Web sites in droves. And, as usual, newspaper executives seem content to make a few dollars simply doing what's good enough to get by. This approach will not do and will not last. The most significant challenge to traditional journalism is coming and will stampede those who are complacent.

Who will construct and manage this new world of mass media? There are disturbing questions here. There are the self-named new media journalists who are gathering speed and skill, art and power online, but sometimes have trouble with the essentials: accuracy, attribution, sourcing, fairness, thoroughness, not to mention solid judgment. Anyone can be a publisher online, it is said, and to some unfortunate extent, this is true. The careless, the vindictive, the cruel and the crazy are there online, sometimes posing as journalists, denigrating centuries of knowledge, damaging with abandon rather than questioning with discipline.

Paradoxically, this is happening as the new media are quietly requiring journalists to reach a standard of excellence that is higher than ever. They are doing so because journalists no longer can say they didn't have space or time for all the quotes, all the documentation, all the **actualities.** There are few limits on news space on the Web, and increasingly the audience is demanding journalists lay out more of the information gathered in the course of good reporting. As all good reporters know, the hardest part of telling a challenging story is knowing what to leave *out,* not what to put *in.*

When you find something on the Web you would like to *get* on your computer's **hard drive** or just as a printout, the process you use is called **downloading.** When you want to *put* information on the Internet, you use a process called **uploading.** The challenges before the journalists of the 21st century are immense. They are as deep and wide as the Web itself, as changing as a breaking story, and as important as the future. What is uploaded today will undoubtedly be downloaded on all of us in the future.

■ What Is a Multimedia Journalism Story?

Multimedia is a hallmark of what will distinguish the news and information of the future. But it is, at first, a sometimes perplexing term.

On the first day of class a brave student raised a hand to ask the question that was on everyone's mind but that nobody wanted to ask: What exactly is a multimedia journalism story? Can it be a feature story, for example, about a growing number of white punk rockers filling in a part of the city's oldest black ghetto? Is it a hard news story about the ongoing budget crisis? Is it a local story about a mail carrier being honored by the Postal Service? Is it a sports story, a business story, an international diplomatic story? The answer, in three unsatisfactory words, is yes and no.

A multimedia journalism story is first and foremost unlike any other story you have ever reported, edited or produced. You must consider—but then put aside—how a newspaper, magazine, TV network or radio station would cover the story. You must think about your story in a new, expansive way that has different boundaries and few precedents.

Let's take the feature story. A newspaper article would describe the ghetto, the boarded-up buildings, the police, the winos and the poor families struggling to make things work despite adversity. It would probably start with an anecdotal lead, a vivid, symbolic vignette a few paragraphs long. The reporter would go to the area and interview a dozen or so people, perhaps bringing a photographer along. A few calls would be made to local officials, as many more would be made to verify facts, and perhaps some special sources would be contacted to add interest and analysis. Then the editor would start barking about this being a daily newspaper and where the hell is that piece.

The reporter would then become a writer, sitting down to tell the story and quickly getting to the **nut graph.** The standard story structure would summarize some of the main points, put a good quote early on, and then embark on the narrative.

If the reporter were lucky enough to get a photographer and some space, two or three good still pictures might be reproduced. A magazine would use a different writing style, of course, but with the same basic format, expanded, and a larger, more layered use of photos.

What if someone at a television station or network saw the newspaper story and thought the basic reporting legwork could be used to knock off a good story for the weekend? What would the elements of the television news story be? It might start with **wide shots** of the most decrepit slums, a lively corner market, crack dealers on another corner. The video could then show the punk rockers, **sound up** on their music and **dissolve** quickly to several **bites** by the main characters in the story. The reporter would do a **stand-up** close and the two minutes would be done.

Radio, if there were a station or network willing to try it, would use a great deal of **natural sound** and actualities.

Now for multimedia's shot at this story. First, try to put aside what print and broadcast would do, at least for the time being. Then sit down, think and sketch out all the potential elements of this story.

Multimedia is visual, so begin by considering visual elements. Would it be best to **spray** the place with video and hope to **stream** it into the site? Should the pictures be in black and white to underscore the dismal feeling of a ghetto or in color to show people there is life and hope and complexity? Maybe both? Should still photography be used to arrest the audience's attention? Maybe both still and video? (Note the semantic shift. No longer are there simply *readers, viewers* or *listeners.* The person the story is being created for is all three and a bit more. *End user* is the computer term, usually shortened to *user.* But as more than one wag has noted, the computer and drug trades are the only two that comfortably call a customer a *user.* For online journalism, the word *audience* is best, reminding journalists that they are storytellers and should be proud of it.)

Next you would consider sound. Rock 'n' roll, naturally. But what about rap, soul, reggae? Opera? Coltrane? A combination? Would it make sense to use the **sound under** the pictures and the text? Where? Should the sound come up to dominate and take over the story? For how long? The use of music immediately raises important questions about intellectual property rights (as will use of any nonoriginal material). Use of music is governed by some of the most stringent copyright laws and it's something online journalists have to deal with right from the beginning. Questions about copyright, trademarks and what journalists can and can't use (until the next court decision) are addressed in Chapter 9.

Sound also raises the question of editorializing, of creating a mood that may not actually exist in an accurate story. Chapter 5 examines this issue in greater detail.

Quotes and soundbites raise more questions. Were the conversations taped? Should they be listened to or read? Would it be best to mix them with music and **cover** with video or a slide show?

What about graphics? Where is the place in the story? Should the story include a map that shows the region, the neighborhood, the street? Should the map move? Should it be static?

The decisions seem endless, which is both the bane and joy of multimedia. The journalist can add as much information and as many layers as necessary to tell the story well. Remember, this medium differs from others in its limits on time and space. There are limits, however, on what the audience will tolerate. Technological problems with such matters as **download time** and browsers are discussed later. Packaging a multimedia story involves three basic levels: a first level, which provides a brief summary that's more than a headline but quickly lets the audience decide whether it wants more of the story; a second level, which opens up the story significantly from the simple headline version; and a third level, which allows the audience to go deep into the story and makes a great deal of in-depth information available if the audience chooses to pursue it.

Let's take a well-known, if not brand new, news story to illustrate these levels, or tiers: the bombing of the federal building in Oklahoma City.

Tier One would be an immediate **news hook** to the story—anything from the **breaking event** itself to news **folos** afterward, such as the trial of the two men charged with the bombing.

For this example, let's assume the story angle is about the similarities between the right-wing extremists of the 1990s and the left-wing extremists of the 1960s. Tier One explains to the audience that this is the story through the headline (or title), the choice of illustrations and the text, which must have a clear, explanatory nut graph. A Tier One approach also gives the audience an opportunity—and incentive—to go on to Tier Two, which is accessed by a **link.**

Links can be dry and simple tools, or they can be used, as in all good storytelling, to *invite* the audience to go on. In developing links, it is important to know the difference between news copy that delivers true information and advertising copy that promises desirable items it can't really deliver. True journalism demands quality and reality but at the same time must be sensitive to the need for keeping the audience interested in the story. This issue is addressed in some depth in Chapter 5.

Tier Two would fully explore the story. In this example, Tier Two might explain that the Students for a Democratic Society had a radical splinter group called the Weathermen, which was blamed for bombing other Americans in the 1960s as a protest against the Vietnam War. Then the story could explore likenesses and differences between groups such as the Weathermen and groups like the Viper Militia, whose members were arrested in Arizona in the late 1990s, angry and violent regarding taxes and gun control.

The story could use photos of the occupation of a building at Columbia University or the University of California at Berkeley in 1966 and the Freemen occupation in Montana in 1996. Chanting at a Vietnam War protest and recordings of political messages sent to right-wing militia groups could be used for sound. And for graphics, a map of the United States could detail politically rationalized bomb blasts over 30 years.

The rest of the story in Tier Two could include photos dissolving into each other of the Oklahoma federal building before and after the bombing; search-and-rescue video; and graphics such as iron crosses and clenched fists. Accompanying sound could be vivid quotes or, better yet, natural sound (sometimes called **wild sound**), such as sounds of paramilitary drills conducted by a group in the story.

Again, it is key in journalism not to make implications or include materials that are not fact-based. Symbols, sounds or other storytelling devices that are not truly reflective of the story do not belong. Adhering to these principles takes discipline and good judgment. Veteran journalists often have as many qualms and doubts and hazy areas as student journalists have, but professionals recognize their doubts and then err on the side of caution. You must also.

Now Tier Three: the in-depth version with the full text and sound from interviews, video to download, a reader **chatroom** or **message board** (once upon a time called **bulletin boards** or **BBS**) and maybe even a scheduled live, online discussion with sources. Tier Three also establishes links that take the audience away from the story and its parent publication. These links serve as an appendix for further explorations outside the disciplined framework of this particular multimedia story.

Links in this case could be to a page thrown up by a right-wing militia or left-wing underground group or to the FBI or instructions on how to use the Freedom of Information Act to get records. The ability to click to see, hear and read more or to send a message to someone in the story provides the audience with an enormous amount of power. The audience might want to link to a history or sociology site that has vastly more information on U.S. violence and politics, dip into census statistics or visit a museum with exhibits on dissent and power. The sky, the size of your server's hard drive—and your time and money—are the usual limits. How many doors do you want to open? Too many links and you can lose the audience to cyberspace, where people will wander, having forgotten (or lost interest in) where they started. Too few, and you haven't taken advantage of the medium. Where do you, the journalist, draw the line?

Welcome to introductory online journalism.

Hardware Needs

The most intimidating aspect of multimedia journalism is not the hard work or the number of people needed for this truly collaborative effort. The first great psychological, financial and time hurdles all involve equipment, also known as *hardware*. The program at San Francisco State started modestly, taking one step at a time, and others can start this way, too.

First comes the computer. In the business, the term *computer* does not include the **monitor** (the screen), the keyboard, the **mouse,** the **modem** or any other attachments (sometimes referred to as **peripherals**). A computer, in the simplest terms, comprises a **hard drive,** a **processor,** and **RAM.** It can be little or big, fast or slow.

With multimedia, the bigger and faster the better. Some of the software programs needed to create and to run multimedia are huge, and they're growing larger with each new version. The computer will need to be able to run programs like Photoshop, Illustrator, SoundEdit and Flash, and for those the computer needs room and speed.

The bottom-line list:

At least 4 **gigabytes** of memory on the hard disk

64 **megabytes** of RAM

400 **MHz** of **processing speed**

If you can afford more or faster, go for it. If you can't, grit your teeth and hope the price of everything keeps dropping. The monitor has to be color and at least 17 inches. The larger the monitor the better, because you're going to be designing, which requires room and the ability to see things in detail. Until recently most designers were using 14-inch screens because that's still what most people have at home or at the office. But designers have found they are able to work better on a larger canvas.

In the excitement of online authoring it's easy to forget that most people have computers, modems and operating speeds a couple of years behind the curve. It is a good idea to post a reminder of the specific download times for computers with standard **33.6K** and **56K** modems. At San Francisco State University they are on the walls of the computer lab, on the machines themselves and in handouts. An easy-to-use table with these numbers is in Chapter 6.

If you are using Macs, it's nice to have some PCs available, as some material will come in formatted for a PC. If you are using PCs, you'll need at least one Mac close by so that you can see how a story will look when it is sent to the other system. (Some very basic background: Macintosh computers are different from Windows **operating systems.** A lot of software can run on both, and software that can is called *cross-platform*. What matters, however, is that people in the audience are using one system or the other and will see the story according to their computer, not yours. In short, you have to design your story so that it looks and sounds and functions the way you want on *both* systems. Another aside: PC stands for *personal computer,* which applies to both systems but has become shorthand for any non-Mac computer. Equally critical differences in browsers are discussed in Chapter 8.)

To enable people to come in and look at the story, a Web server is necessary. You can create one, but the capacity of the computer will limit the number of people who can simultaneously read or look at your story. Again, the bigger, the better. A decent-sized multimedia site requires a dedicated server.

Think of the Web server as the printing press and you will begin to appreciate the enormity of its significance. All the best reporting, writing, pictures and sound in the world mean nothing if people can't see it. The server does something profoundly simple: it serves up content to those seeking it. If the audience can't get access to your **site,** what's the point? The program at San Francisco State uses a server made by Intergraph, which meets the requirements of being reliable and expandable (**scalable** in computer talk).

An online journalism lab also needs a teaching station, a good printer, a flatbed color scanner, a VCR, a tape deck and a CD player. At some point, reporting tools such as video cameras and tape recorders will be desired. (Decent digital cameras, both video and still, are expensive, but like so much digital technology, they are dropping significantly in price. They may be added to a wish list. Digital cameras allow you to put images directly into the computer without messing with a conversion process, and the result is images of significantly better quality. The data is easier to use, especially in the editing process, and digital is becoming standard in the news industry.)

For the lab at San Francisco State we decided on Macintosh computers because much multimedia authoring is done on Macs and the Mac is an easier, more elegant and more efficient machine than the PC. At the beginning of the Web's popularity the majority of multimedia software was written originally for Macs, but this is no longer the case. However, many professional multimedia designers still compare Macs to Acuras and PCs to Chevys—not that there is anything wrong with Chevys. If you don't have a lot of cash at purchase time and you do have a lot of time to fix them and a lot of patience, they may be for you.

It is important to note, though, that good PCs are getting more like Macs in ways that make the choices far less important today than they

The Macintosh computer made by Apple differs in many important ways, in addition to appearance, from the more common non-Macs, usually referred to as *PCs*. Pictured here are the Mac G4 and a high-end Web PC from Dell.

Macintosh computer image used with the permission of Apple Computers and Mark Laita Photography. Copyright © by Mark Laita Photography. Dell computer image used with the permission of Dell Computer Corporation.

were a few years ago. And the emerging changes in programming (explained later) may make many differences immaterial. That will be a wonderful development. But don't hold your breath. It won't be overnight.

■ Software Needs

If the hardware is the body of the equipment, the software is the central nervous system. (Journalists still have to provide the thinking with real brains—sometimes referred to by computer geeks as *wetware*.) Software changes all the time. That's one reason Bill Gates keeps getting richer. It's also the reason some people shy away from learning the basics; they believe that as soon as they master one set of tools, those tools will become obsolete. There is a bit of truth in this, but only a bit.

Generally, learning current software is an excellent avenue to knowing the new version arriving next year, next month, maybe tomorrow. If you know Photoshop 6.0, you'll learn the next version quickly and be grateful for having mastered its extra powers in short order.

A less tangible advantage of this knowledge is that once you learn how to use some of these key pieces of software you'll realize that just about anyone can and that multimedia creation is not only for computer programmers. In the past plenty of newspeople refused to learn how to use telephones, typewriters and word processors. Imagine what would have happened to the news industry if reporters had not taken control of these essential tools of the last 100 years!

The following elements are basic to online journalism production. First, you need to know basic **Hypertext Markup Language (HTML).** This is not a significant challenge, and it's getting easier all the time. HTML is used to create Web pages, and it's central to online journalism. Several new software programs known as HTML editors have been developed to help create Web pages (Dreamweaver and FrontPage are two examples), but none offer the ability to do really interesting and unique things with a page. Most sites constructed with a **graphical** HTML editor have a cookie-cutter look, having come from pretty much the same mold. Another option is a program like BBEdit, which allows a great deal more flexibility while creating shortcuts to writing HTML code.

Regardless of the approach taken, learning to write basic HTML, either from one of the many books available or from one of the tutorial sites on the Web, is a task that requires several days. Some of the best tutorial sites can be found in our Online Workbook.

The software will quickly improve, and at some point in the distant future a hands-on knowledge of HTML may not be necessary. But for now, it is vital to learn the basics in order to design pages that will actually help tell the story. It's also important for the journalist to have the power over the code, rather than vice versa. This issue is addressed more in Chapter 2.

Next on the list of basics is Photoshop, a widely used graphics program by Adobe. Most people in media production are familiar with Photoshop as software that puts together images for everything from newspapers to brochures, but it's much more than that. It is a crucial piece of software used to create graphics, import photos, and structure much of the artwork for your story. It's the first piece of software you have to learn, and it's central to multimedia stories.

People can take this software as deep as time and talent will allow. Some people become wizards much as others are wizards with cameras, sound or database construction.

You, however, need only know Photoshop well enough to make it work for you in telling a story and to be able to ask intelligent and knowledgeable questions about how to construct the story in optimal fashion. The same logic applies to the other software programs with which you need to be familiar. It's somewhat like learning conversational Spanish—one can function fairly well with a basic knowledge, aware that time and experience will bring a greater degree of fluency.

Alongside Photoshop is Adobe's Illustrator, an art program capable of creating rather sophisticated graphics. An introductory level of understanding of this program is very helpful.

At San Francisco State, we used to require students to learn to download video using a program such as Premiere and to bring audio to stories using SoundEdit to create, alter or place sounds in the story. We have placed these a little to the side with the rapid advances of a technology known as streaming. Streaming video and audio allows the audience to start hearing and listening to aspects of the story as it is downloading, as opposed to having to wait for an entire **file** to download before it becomes accessible. More advanced students may look to Java or the more accessible Java Scripting. A fast-growing number of multimedia authors are increasingly using a tool called Flash, which allows them to combine text, video, sounds and animation into an overall package with relatively small **file sizes.**

A Century Closes, a Century Opens

LARRY PRYOR

In only the last five years of the last century, online journalism grew into the most powerful medium since the first live radio broadcast in 1920. Some nine million computers were connected to the Internet in 1995, with an audience that was mostly made up of educated, affluent men in the United States. By 2000, more than 122 million computers were hooked up worldwide. Surveys showed that the audience had become mainstream and had a strong interest in news.

A study by the Pew Research Center for the People and the Press found in 1999 that online news attracted 36 million weekly readers, or triple the number of three years earlier. Young people in particular used the Internet as a news source. And by 2000, more than 60 percent of U.S. newspapers had Web sites, the top ones getting more than three million unique visits per month. Broadcast network sites, such as CNN's, were ranked among the most-used sites. Some content providers were beginning to move beyond the Web to new digital and wireless platforms. The popularity of general-interest topics—local and entertainment news, sports and weather information—continued to grow exponentially.

The new medium had proved itself to be portable, interactive, real-time and limitless in its depth of content. And although much of that content had been derived from other media, mostly newspapers and network TV, by the end of 1999 more news Web sites were creating content specifically for the Web. Reporters at major papers, such as The New York Times, Washington Post and Chicago Tribune, for example, had begun to file news stories directly to their Web sites, breaking the established print news cycle of one major edition per day.

Those sorts of numbers taken together would lead most analysts to say the future of online journalism is assured. It may not be.

This fast growth has occurred in a swirl of controversy. No medium could be expected to grow so quickly, displacing use of other media and breaking reader habits, without drawing scrutiny and criticism. Independent Web columnist Matt Drudge became the symbol of the gossip and unverified news tips that swirled across the Internet. This material was often picked up by traditional media without further checking, which amplified the problem. But Drudge's revelations about Monica Lewinsky in 1998, lifted from Newsweek's reporting in advance of publication by the magazine, proved to be accurate. Was Newsweek correct in holding on to the story? Probably. Will the experience make real journalists more sensitive to competition? Certainly.

Much of the subsequent coverage of the Clinton scandal, although salacious and sensational, was eagerly consumed by the new Web audience. Major news events such as the death of Princess Diana, the 1998 elections and the release of the Staff Report drew mass numbers of readers to news Web sites, and the medium became legitimate, an integral part of many people's lives. Press critics such as James Fallows acknowledged, "Real journalism is being practiced there [on the Web]."

Traditional print and broadcast editors, publishers and network executives suddenly found they had to take note of the public's appetite for online news. In the meantime, new Web sites had developed with no ties to existing news organizations. Some covered a particular niche of news, such as technology, sports or finance. Others, such as Salon and Slate, resembled magazines. Many catered to specific audiences, such as expectant mothers or health enthusiasts, and offered editorial content closely tied to e-commerce. The new entrepreneurs found they could enter the medium at a relatively modest cost and that their growth prospects worldwide were virtually unlimited.

The valuations placed on news and information sites by Wall Street investors were astronomical. Companies such as AOL, which was an online pioneer, saw their wealth grow by 5,000 to 6,000 percent during the 1990s. This economic growth carried a distinct threat for newspapers, which began to see their classified ads migrate to the Internet. They also saw a growing number of the editorial staff move into jobs at Web sites, where the pay scale was far higher and the atmosphere for innovation more attractive.

Traditional media managers began either to invest more heavily in their own new media properties or to join with entrepreneurs native to the Web. Acquisitions, mergers and partnerships became the financial news of the day as the 20th century drew to a close. This raised the possibility that Web news would become dominated by the same companies that dominated other forms of media.

Despite the entry of conglomerates into online journalism, the growth of Web and wireless news sites continued at a frenzied pace. Credible news content became a valued commodity. E-commerce sites that were driven by marketing concerns suddenly began to hire journalists and ask them to erect walls between sales and editorial staffs.

The new medium placed emphasis on design and coherent navigation, calling for new skills from journalists. News reports on the Web became more of a multimedia presentation as software improved and the capacity to deliver data to homes and offices improved. Online journalists had to learn new tools. Computer-assisted reporting became important both for traditional investigations and for the delivery of information in new ways online.

As one century closed and a new century opened, it remained to be seen whether these new trends would go unchecked or whether the success of technology would provoke a counterreaction. As the new medium also has the potential for misuse, concerns about censorship, propaganda, violations of privacy and intellectual property rights have become major concerns worldwide. The future of new media seems bright, but such spectacular growth brings with it many liabilities and painful economic and social adjustments.

Larry Pryor directs the Online Program at the Annenberg School for Communication at the University of Southern California in Los Angeles and is on the Journalism School faculty. He was a reporter for the Louisville Courier-Journal and then for the Los Angeles Times, where he later held various editing positions, including editor of the Times' Web site.

chapter 2

Day One

> *When a reporter sits down at the*
> *typewriter, he's nobody's friend.*
> —Theodore White

You begin by sitting in front of the keyboard, monitor and computer; you stretch your arms, glance out the window and look at the clock. Time to get started. But how? Where? What's the next step?

Like the newsmen and newswomen at the beginning of the 20th century sitting down to tell a story on a typewriter, journalists first have to learn to type. Today, most people type with ease. The task that faces the journalist now is to type simple computer codes in a very learnable language called HTML. After some basic familiarity with that task is achieved, the journalist heads for the challenge of creating good story ideas that can be expressed in a multimedia fashion. Day one begins.

It's time to begin exploring and creating. The first tasks are as important as the last. The basic language of writing on the World Wide Web, HTML, is not really a language of its own, as computer-programming languages are normally regarded. Strictly speaking, it is called computer code—and the people who do it well are called coders. You don't need to be a professional coder to be an online journalist, but you mustn't be afraid of learning the basics. People drawn to journalism often feel anxious when someone suggests they learn how to create links through HTML. After all, if they wanted to be computer coders, they would have majored in computer sciences, right?

Learning HTML is an all-important bridge journalists must cross. It is not much different from the bridge they cross when they learn how to type, when they learn to ask people in power to respond to a revelation of their dishonesty, when they learn how to recognize a **jump cut.** It is part of a basic skill set for the next generation of journalists. Simply put, HTML is the new grammar.

A basic tutorial in HTML is essential because it will enable you to understand the blueprint of the site-construction process, to ask the right sorts of questions during the construction phase and to engineer your story with precision and individuality.

A parallel concept in traditional newspaper journalism would be a working understanding of page layout; in television news, it would be learning the basic structure of video editing. In large news operations, these tasks are left to specialists—creating a gap in knowledge felt by those not fortunate enough to have begun with small organizations—but truly good editors and producers understand enough to ensure quality.

It's fun to listen to TV news veterans talk nostalgically about the good old days when they had to shoot on film, edit their own stories, write and then anchor live shots. But the reality is that the production values were so primitive that it was a hard medium to watch for any period of time. And, nostalgia aside, the process no doubt required a great deal of very stressful effort.

A day will come in online journalism when a journalist will become a real producer without having developed a thorough set of multimedia authoring skills. But it hasn't arrived yet, and it won't for quite some time.

The New Grammar

HTML is more tedious than difficult. It's easier to learn than driving a car, and a lot safer. By simply typing certain codes—or what Web authors call **tags**—into a story you can create the basic language for World Wide Web pages.

It is best to begin writing for the World Wide Web using what Web authors call raw HTML, rather than using software such as HTML editors that do some or much of the work for you. Think of it as learning to bake a cake from scratch rather than from a mix. At some point you might want to use a mix to save time, but you should know the essential ingredients you are using. What if you wanted a slight coconut flavor that wasn't in the mix? You would have to settle for something you didn't want.

Starting from scratch means not using word processing programs, such as Word, because they won't work for you. Instead, begin with a text-only program, such as Simple Text or Notepad. Another common way to refer to text only is **ASCII** (pronounced "ASK-ee"). We use BBEdit, made for writing HTML tags.

Perhaps you want to write something basic, such as "Police Arrest Man." You want this sentence to appear in HTML so you can post it on the World Wide Web. Despite the mystery surrounding this process, it will be among the easiest things you have ever done. First you'll write the sentence in a text-only format, then you'll type a few simple characters (tags) in the proper place and see what happens. The most basic tags are angled brackets and slashes on either side of some basic letters.

First type: Police Arrest Man.

Save the page or document.

Now type `<HTML>` before the word *Police.*

Now type `</HTML>` after the word *Man.*

By putting this simple code in the Netscape or Internet Explorer program you'll see that you have created a Web page.

Naturally, there is much more to this process. The online site provides step-by-step instructions as well as a list of Web sites that will take you through as much HTML as you need or want. The most basic and essential tags you'll need to know are the following:

```
<HTML>  </HTML>
<TITLE>  </TITLE>
<HEAD>  </HEAD>
<BODY>  </BODY>
<P>
<BR>
<LI>  </UL>
```

Learning the basics of simple HTML is the first step toward mastering one of the most elegant, powerful and far-reaching tools of mass communication since the telephone: the **hyperlink.** The all-important tag that actually creates links looks like this:

```
<A HREF="URL">text</A>
```

The hyperlink will be discussed throughout this introduction to online journalism. Remember, there are programs that attempt to do all the coding for the user. As these programs improve, the amount of tedious coding you'll have to do for each page will decrease. For now, though, you are concerned with convenience and speed versus flexibility and completeness. The essential idea is to be able, in short order, to create a Web site that will leave room to grow and experiment.

There is an abundance of books and Web sites that offer help learning layouts, gimmicks, shortcuts and ambitious ways to squeeze the most out of Web pages. Two of the best for people building Web pages are Web Monkey (http://www.hotwired.com/webmonkey) and Builder.com (http://www.builder.com). They are both clear and up to date and have e-mail lists that

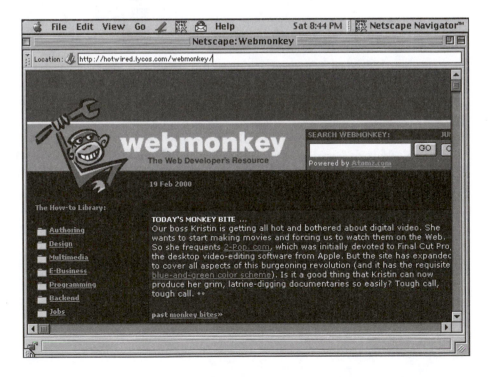

Although there are countless Web sites with great information online on how to build Web pages and troubleshoot them (see the Online Workbook for some we particularly like), two of the most popular overall sites for Web building are WebMonkey.com and Builder.com, shown here.

WebMonkey Web page used with permission. Copyright © 1994–2000 by Wired Digital, Inc., a Lycos Network company. All rights reserved. CNET Builder.com Web page used with permission. Copyright © 1995–2000 by CNET Networks, Inc.

regularly send subscribers step-by-step information on how to build and improve their work. They are, like most Web sites, free. "Writers working in this medium," says Steve Outing of Editor & Publisher and Planetary News (http://www.planetarynews.com), "need to understand and keep up with the technological developments—at the least, to understand what's possible." The payoff is significant, because the more you learn, the more powerful you become.

When your story is done and loaded onto an active file or Web server—another computer with special software to handle multiple incoming and outgoing signals—it becomes part of the World Wide Web. Millions of people across the planet will be able to see the story at astounding speeds.

HTML homework involves getting on the computer and using a tutorial to create a simple set of pages. The best way to start is by constructing a page about you. In Web parlance this is called a vanity page, and there are thousands of them out there. You've no doubt seen Web pages with pictures of the authors' pets, descriptions of their cars, lists of their favorite bands. These pages are often banal and rarely illuminating. Still, there are good reasons to start this way. First, you know the topic (remember the axiom of writing about what you know). Second, it's a sound idea for everyone—and especially for students—to build an electronic resume.

You can create secondary pages that contain more specialized information (employment history or a collection of family photos, as serious or weird as you like) and link those pages to your **home page.** Links going back to the home page are often labeled "Home." (A quick note about privacy: Never post anything on the Web that you wouldn't mind posted on your school or company bulletin board, because the Web is the biggest and most accessible bulletin board ever. The same advice goes for e-mail.) Then, you can create hyperlinks among the pages. Once you've done that, you're in business.

Naturally there is a great deal to all this. Just as naturally, there will be limits to your time, patience and, maybe, abilities. Designing Web pages is sort of like learning to play racquetball: easy and fun to learn the basics, hard but rewarding to master. As with most worthwhile enterprises, the learning never stops. Webmasters who have been designing and building complicated pages for years learn new tags and tricks all the time. Like all great achievers, from open-heart surgeons to videogame warriors, the best Web authors consider the challenge and the learning some of the primary attractions.

Part of the process of mastering Web-authoring skills is to observe and study other Web sites, news and otherwise, seeing what works, what doesn't and what simply intrigues. Begin by finding and critiquing 10 Web sites that have something to do with journalism. If you've been on the Web for a while you'll be rolling your eyes at this. But it's not a make-work assignment. Each site should be analyzed using a series of key questions:

- What makes it journalism?
- Was the information credible and verifiable?
- Was the information useful?
- Was it interesting?
- What elements of multimedia did the site use?
- Was the information arranged logically?
- Did you find what you were looking for?
- Was anything confusing?
- What will you remember from this site in two weeks?
- What would have made this site better?

The Online Workbook has links to some of the best, most imaginative and interesting Web sites for online journalists. The Workbook also provides clear guidelines about what to look for.

Reconciling Experts and Amateurs

For the pioneer online journalism production course at San Francisco State University, we deliberately recruited students who were not on the **Net** and who didn't even have e-mail accounts. The intent was to avoid straying too far away from a mass media audience, for the mass media have much more direct contact with what truly works in multimedia storytelling.

It's all too easy in journalism to forget what is interesting and important to people from many walks of life, and that is a fatal trap for people in the news business. Online journalism faces new dangers because journalists can quickly learn Web authoring and just as quickly forget that they are doing it for the people who click onto their sites—not for students, professors or Web coders.

Students who are beginners and students who are already computer literate both create their own learning curves, mostly straight up. And they all have something to teach their classmates, if not about computers, then about news value, or writing skills or sourcing. Nearly everyone in the online journalism production course plays both student and teacher, and the non-technical people have a great deal to offer. It is obviously crucial that novices in Web authoring listen and learn from students with advanced skills. But it is equally crucial for the advanced coders to pay attention to the novices as they react to what makes for clear and compelling storytelling. This is the beginning of something rather intangible, but essential to a successful online enterprise: cooperation.

Online journalism is a radical departure from print journalism (and rather more like broadcast news) in that it is a highly collaborative affair. Newspaper reporters are often the owner-operators of their stories, but no one person can create sustained, quality online journalism. With print journalism, the reporter files a story and leaves, an editor fixes and rewrites the story and leaves, a layout person aligns it correctly on a page and goes home. With online journalism there is serious, active cooperation at every turn.

Naturally, tempers can flare, especially in the course of producing a creative, enterprising piece of work under a deadline. The distinguishing difference between an amateur and a professional reporter is the ability to handle the pressure and complete the task with grace. The basic rule among pros is simple: When conflicts arise, forget about what's best for you and honestly focus on *what's best for the story.* Nine times out of 10, even the most passionate people will come to an understanding, remembering that compromise means getting something, but also giving up something.

Every person in an online journalism production class must have an e-mail account. Most universities and colleges provide an e-mail system at little or no cost. Many students prefer to use a **Commercial Service Provider,** such as America Online, or one of the many direct ramps to the Net, called **Internet Service Providers (ISPs).**

All systems have advantages and disadvantages. Some schools' systems have quickly become overloaded with accounts, and with some systems it seems to take forever simply to log on. Bills for commercial service providers with hourly rates can be surprisingly large. Nonetheless, a system is necessary. The key here is for students to become comfortable with communicating online. They'll need to use the Net for the class, for doing research (it's an interview tool, somewhere between mailing surveys and using the phone), and for filing excuses with the instructor.

It's not necessary to use the same ISP forever, although changing ISPs is only a little more complicated than changing long-distance telephone providers. It is recommended, though, to have an e-mail address that will remain the same for years. Having to notify everyone about an address

- DSP Communications
  www.dsp.net
- Hypnovista Software
  www.hypno.com
- One IPNet
  www.1ipnet.net
- LaunchNet, Inc.
  www.launchnet.com
- Bay Area InfoServe, Inc.
  www.bais.com
- Grin Net, LLC
  www.grin.net
- Wombat Internet Guild, Inc.
  www.batnet.com
- Tsoft
  www.tsoft.net
- Pacific Bell Internet
  www.pacbell.net
- Faster Than Light
  www.ftl.net
- Your No-Nonsense Network
  www.ynn.net
- Master Link, Inc.
  www.master-link.com
- Prado Internet Access, Inc.
  www.prado.com
- NetWizards, Inc.
  www.netwiz.net
- InReach Internet, Inc.
  www.inreach.com
- Catapult Integrated Systems
  www.catapult.net

- MagicLink Internet Services
  www.magiclink.net
- World Internet System Resources
  www.wisr.net
- GPL Internet
  www.gplbbs.com
- Zytek Communications Corp.
  www.zytek.com
- I-Step Communications
  www.istep.com
- Infoasis
  www.infoasis.com
- LineX Communications
  linex.com
- GoldState.net
  www.cwo.net
- Activa.Net
  www.activa.net
- Creative Strategies
  www.creative.net
- ViaNet Communications
  www.via.net
- Transport Logic
  www.transport.com
- Electric Lightwave, Inc.
  www.eli.net
- Hodge Interactive Productions
  www.hodge.com
- AccessPort
  www.ap.net
- Globix Corp.
  www.globix.com

continues

There are thousands of Internet Service Providers (ISPs) across the nation and the world that you can use to get on the Internet. These are just a few from a very long list posted on the Web for the 415 area code (San Francisco). Most charge about $20 a month for unlimited access to the Web, but the business is competitive with many good deals to be found.

- ImaginOn, Inc.
  www.inow.com

- San Francisco Legal Network
  www.sflegal.net

- AmerNet
  www.amer.net

- Byte Communications
  www.bytenet.com

- Sine Wave Solutions, LLC
  www.sinewave.com

- Monarch Communications, Inc.
  www.monarchcom.net

- Internet Sphere Interactive, Inc.
  www.i-sphere.com

- Diamond Lane, The
  www.tdl.com

- Webbnet
  www.webbnet.com

- Infinex Telecom, Inc.
  www.infinex.com

- C2 Technologies
  www.c2technology.com

- Meer.net
  www.meer.net

- Winterlink, Inc.
  www.winterlink.net

- Augur, Inc.
  www.augur.com

- The-City.com
  www.the-city.com

- Internet 2xtreme
  www.2xtreme.net

- Direct Network Access, Ltd.
  www.dnai.com

- Virtual Sites, Inc.
  www.v-site.net

- BayLinks Communications
  www.baylinks.com

- ISP Networks, Inc.
  www.isp.net

- Internet Frontier
  www.internet-frontier.net

- Fabrik Communications, Inc.
  www.fabrik.com

- Pathlink Technology Corp.
  www.pathlink.net

- San Francisco Personal Computer
  Users Group
  www.sfpcug.org

- Zoom.Com Information Services, Inc.
  www.zoom.com

- CaliforniaCom, Inc.
  www.california.com

- Value Net Internetwork Services, Inc.
  www.value.net

- ZCO Internet Solutions
  www.zco.net

- A-Link Network Services, Inc.
  www.alink.net

- Tomato Web Online
  www.tomatoweb.com

- WebPerception
  www.webperception.com

- Idiom Consulting
  www.idiom.com

- Mendocino Community Network
  www.mcn.org

change is rarely quick or painless. Yet if those notifications aren't made, many opportunities, very much including career moves, are likely to be lost. It is almost inevitable that you will have to change e-mail addresses as you move along your career path. A constant address, which can serve as a central receiving station to which other addresses *forward* mail, is invaluable. Forwarding is a simple and immensely practical way for journalists to stay in touch with all the matters you need to stay close to. Free, lifetime e-mail is available through many services, such as Yahoo! Mail, Hotmail and Excite Mail.

How to Get Started Without Tripping at the Start Line

The next step, which needs to be made almost immediately, is generating story ideas. This is pure journalism, which must keep pace with the technical side. You should begin by generating at least three ideas for stories that will employ multimedia: text, sound, visuals, interactivity. Beginning journalism students tend to be preoccupied with stories that are *not* stories, but topics. For example, it is not uncommon for novice students of journalism to suggest (or in the argot of the newsroom "pitch") a story about the state of environmentalism. There are, however, some basic definitions of *news*. These definitions are broad enough to allow tremendous creativity but specific enough to be both focused and workable. These guidelines have been fought and won over many years and should not be discarded lightly.

Deciding what is news has baffled, intrigued and fired up journalists since the beginning.

A very basic place to start is: *News is what's interesting and what's important.* Mature journalists may recognize this definition as almost deceptively simple but will agree it's a good starting point. The more a story has of both what's interesting and what's important, the better it is. Stories about the International Monetary Fund may be far more important than interesting, but the role of the journalist is to make the story as interesting as possible. Stories about the Kennedys may be more interesting than important, which leaves reporters anxiously trying to make them also seem important. A story that is naturally chock full of both attributes is a page one, top-of-the-segment, lead story.

The long debate over what is news is usually instructive and often amusing. Suggestions over the years have run the gamut, from the wonderfully irreverent "women, wampum and wrongdoing," attributed to former

New York Times City Editor Stanley Walker, to the standard (and widely attributed) "When a dog bites a man, that's *not* news. When a man bites a dog, that *is* news."

It is unfailingly helpful to remember the obvious: *News is new.* News is contingent on something happening. In journalism terms, a story is news if it has a **news hook** or trigger. There must be a *new* aspect to this action or it simply is not news. That's that.

Along the same lines, the very best of the journalistic breed fully understand that their work is distinguished by the originality of their stories—their **scoops** or beats as they are sometimes called. A tried-and-true method of testing the quality of a newspaper, broadcast outlet or online journalism site is to measure how many truly new, original stories are evident. The following chapter will spend more time on this vitally important trait.

Stories can be **hard news** or **news features,** analytic or just plain fun. But they must all have basic news value. If you can't capture a significant number of imaginations, have a clear grasp of the story's significance and describe in a paragraph what's new about the story—try again. The next chapter will address these issues in greater depth also.

The importance of learning how to come up with original, working story ideas cannot be overestimated, although it is sometimes overlooked by journalism, broadcast and communications departments. Learning to recognize and to *create* top-flight stories is one of the most valuable lessons that define real journalism. It will also be a crucial component in defining online journalism if online journalism is to avoid the tarpit of shovelware, or the more euphemistic term *repurposed content.*

Journalism's most noble mission has been to illuminate darkened corners of the world, believing that destructive viruses prosper in dank, ill-lit environments. Shining a light on the same old places, such as meetings and studies, without true enterprise reporting is poor journalism indeed. And as the standards for meeting obligations grow, so must the journalist's skills.

There is an often heard, though rarely thought out, critique that too much news is negative. This is a conversation that many journalists themselves have failed to engage in, making us all the poorer. Engaging in thoughtful exchange about this issue will give journalists better focus on their tasks as journalists.

"In the old days men had the rack. Now they have the press." This phrase, written by Oscar Wilde a long time ago, remains insightful today. The wordier version is this: We have unspoken social contracts by which we live and prosper. We expect airline pilots to be sober when they fly; we expect politicians to be honest, and we expect journalists to be accurate. When this contract is breached—when a plane crashes, a president prevaricates, a reporter wins a Pulitzer Prize for a fabricated story—that's news.

Do not shy away from story ideas because they are negative. To the contrary, bringing the bright light of public scrutiny to an injustice is a fundamentally positive act. Journalists draw attention to tears in the social fabric because if they do not, their very existence is threatened. This is a slightly more complicated, but primary, definition of the essence of the craft of journalism.

This ethic is as fundamental to online journalism as it is to other media, although but there are some unique differences in its application to online journalism. The online medium has a power of unparalleled reach, scope and speed. Consequently, it must be used with great respect.

Universal stories have far-reaching interest. Such stories are well suited for online journalism because the Web knows no distance and has a flexible sense of time. Yet local stories are more practical to undertake and, ironically, local sites are one of the fastest growing segments of the Web. You may be able to fashion a mix of local and universal stories. Whatever the focus, the key is to remember that this is multimedia and the boundaries must be pushed. Timeworn ways of telling stories must be cast aside in favor of approaches that simply cannot be offered in the old media.

The charter class in online journalism production at San Francisco State University had trouble grasping this concept until one student pitched a story that created an epiphany for the whole group. The stories that were being tossed around in discussion included standard undergraduate topics of drugs, fashions and the environment. And, of course, the Internet. Then one student very quietly said she wanted to take an interesting, yet-to-be-decided subject in the news and throw it to three artists: a painter, a poet and a musician. They would all respond in their own medium and exclusively in that medium: The painter would create an illustration, the poet would use words and the musician would compose and play a special score. They would respond to one another, and there would be no narrative. It was a feature piece, but defiantly multimedia.

Everyone stared at the student, stunned for a moment. Was that journalism? The idea was interesting and would deal with a true news topic in an unusual way. The story would use a set of highly structured interviews, pumped through a technology that allowed one medium to respond directly to another. The front page of this story would tell the audience immediately what it was about and there would be editorial control over the content. Journalistically, it would fly.

The students looked at one another and then the exclamations spurted out. It was almost possible to see them throwing out their old story ideas, their old notions of what could be reported, and start reconstructing from the ground up. Some students, of course, felt frustrated and stumped by the concept of multimedia journalism. One hardworking student came back day after day with story ideas that just would not work—old stories seen in other places, topics without news hooks and sometimes ideas that were just plain boring and insignificant. One day he went on a walk across campus with an instructor, who asked the student if he worked. He did, at a large hotel in downtown San Francisco that had a large and prosperous Japanese tourist clientele. The instructor asked whether the student had anything to tell his friends and family about after work each day. Aside from the wooden toilet seats, the student replied, nothing much. The wooden toilet seats?

The student explained that an inordinate number of the Asian visitors brought large, completely empty suitcases with them, which they filled with wooden toilet seats prior to returning home. The conversation led to a fully formed story pitch about the sorts of strange, small and unnoticed goods in the United States were attracting foreign visitors.

Several years later, a student from Denmark said she wanted to do a story about San Francisco's troubled public transit system, known as Muni. The instructors objected, saying it had been covered extensively and well by local media, it was too provincial and it would not lend itself to the full multimedia environment on the Web. The student explained that the story would center on a moment during a night ride on a San Francisco trolley (not a cable car, but another, more commuter-oriented, light-rail vehicle used extensively in San Francisco). For that one moment, people who come from widely disparate pasts and go off to widely disparate futures are all together, joined in a single purpose, in transit from one point of their lives to another. The story would have many dynamic elements and would be—as almost all great stories are—about people.

Most of the stories finally selected for the online journalism production course are reasonably complex and ambitious and require a good deal of work. For some participants, the idea of true collaboration as a key component to success can be disturbing in the beginning, but liberating at the end.

Teams of two and three students are assigned to each approved story. Each student has to know and understand what the others are doing; each must appreciate the individual strengths brought to the project. Upper-division journalism students are purposely paired with novices. Web authors are coupled with people who don't know a byte from a bite. Brash young students team up with quiet, more mature partners. Just like the real world.

The results are often rather impressive. Online journalism makes professional, intellectual and artistic demands on these students. What they don't expect, many later say, is the extraordinary amount of fun and serious satisfaction that comes with their creations. Although new technologies can frighten away some of the very people they must attract to keep quality journalism thriving, a little patience and open-mindedness will help allay those anxieties. The pieces are in place: the tools, the ideas and the spirit. It is time to move on toward the heart of the great enterprise that lies ahead.

Transforming Journalism Education

JOHN V. PAVLIK

New media, or emerging digital communication and computing technologies, present a fundamental challenge to journalism education. Most programs in journalism education, especially those in the United States, are built around an industrial-age analog media system divided along the lines of content distribution and presentation. As a result, most programs offer courses and concentrations in broadcast (including television and radio), print (including newspaper and magazine) and now, new media, or online journalism. In many cases, courses on new media, or online journalism, are additions to a set of courses or a concentration, complementary to the existing curricula or concentrations.

In other words, despite the emergence of digital communication and computing technologies that are inexorably altering the journalism landscape in all media, many journalism education programs are not taking the opportunity to reexamine and perhaps reinvent their curricula for the next century by integrating new media into all aspects of the journalism curriculum. Instead, many programs are adapting in minimalist fashion, choosing to view the new media simply as a new means of information delivery and presentation.

Although this pedagogical framework may have worked well in preparing students for careers in analog media or for developing media-based analysis and literacy, it bears increasingly little relevance to the emerging digital media system.

In this emerging system, virtually the entire journalistic process is becoming digital, from the acquisition of information (what is referred to as reporting or news gathering), to the storage, indexing and retrieval of that information (text, audio or video), to the production and editing of that content, to its distribution, and finally to the public's access to and interaction with that content and with the journalist. New media represent far more than a new means of content distribution. In the very near term, journalists will use digital tools almost exclusively for the entire journalistic enterprise.

An increasing number of digital tools are already used by news organizations around the world. From the New York Times on the Web, which delivers news to portable digital appliances (e.g., the Palm III), to the Chicago Tribune Company, whose reporters now work in combined newsrooms featuring print, television, online and other means of news delivery, to CNN, with a central newsroom that manages the entire flow of news through a half-dozen news networks from television to the Internet, an increasing number of leading news organizations recognize and are exploiting the potential of these new media tools by reinventing their newsrooms and news products for a digital media environment.

The newly launched Pixelon.com, like a growing number of other Internet *Webcasters* (such as Digital Bitcasting, which streams online via Real Networks or Windows Media Player) delivers broadcast-quality video and audio programming on demand over the Internet. Broadcast quality is defined here as at least 24 frames per second of full-screen video with at least the resolution of VHS tape, with near-CD quality sound (what is known in the online vernacular as MP3). The user needs a high-bandwidth connection to the Internet to receive this broadcast-quality content.

High-bandwidth, or broadband, is at least 300 kilobits per second or higher. This is the type of Internet service provided by cable modems, digital subscriber lines, or DirecPC—the satellite delivery service provided by DirecTV.

As growing numbers of Americans get high-speed Internet access, the delivery of broadcast-quality audio and video via online media will become increasingly commonplace and the control traditional broadcasters exercise over the media's distribution of audio and video will erode substantially, if not disappear entirely. Soon, just as MP3 (the audio-storage file format popular for digital music) has begun to transform the music distribution business, the world of television broadcasting will be transformed by Internet Webcasting. In this world of on-demand media, journalism will feature a rich blend of text, audio, video and interactivity to tell virtually any story. To work effectively in this environment, journalists will need to be comfortable with, if not fluent in, the grammar of all media modalities.

Consider the following stories, which ran in the New York Times in November 1999:

"Beneath Desert, a Majestic Cavern Is Unveiled," a report about Kartchner Caverns, a 550-acre park about 50 miles southeast of Tucson, Arizona

"New Debate on Submarine Duty for Women," a report about women serving on nuclear submarines in the U.S. Navy

"Stealing Millennial Loot in Israel, From 2 Millenniums Ago," a report about modern-day grave robbing in the Judean foothills

Each featured extensive reporting and text-based stories accompanied by some photographs. As well reported as they were, however, each illustrates the potential for using a wider array of storytelling tools to enrich a report. Tools such as 360-degree video, 3D imagery and audio of sources and ambient sound, among others would help bring these reports alive and engage the reader in ways standard reporting simply cannot.

Interactivity and customization are other important features increasingly possible in the digital, online world of 21st-century journalism. Consider the campaign finance page created in 1999 by Politics.com (http://www.politics.com/money/money_frame.cfm). By accessing public data from the Federal Election Commission the site can provide names of donors and amounts donated to each candidate in the 2000 campaign for any zip code in the United States. It can search and sort in a number of other ways as well. This new form of journalism is possible only through digital, online technology. Every journalist and journalism student should understand the fundamental capabilities of these tools.

This digital transformation mandates a fundamental restructuring of journalism education. This restructuring should not be viewed as a threat, although many teachers will view it as such because it represents a major change in how and what they have been teaching. Rather, this transformation should be viewed as an opportunity, perhaps an unprecedented opportunity, for journalism and for the industry known collectively as the media or news business to assume a position of leadership in society. Journalism educators can take this opportunity to reinvent the enterprise of journalism education and lead a troubled industry into a renaissance.

The growth of digital, online media is much more than a new means of information delivery, and online journalism should be more than just another course in an already overcrowded journalism curriculum. A new, integrated journalism curriculum needs to teach students the principles, practices, values and standards of news reporting that cut across media boundaries and embrace interactivity. Students should not learn to be newspaper, magazine, television, radio or online reporters, but should learn to be journalists working in a digital age.* They need to think "outside the box" so that they can create compelling stories for any medium, using the range of modalities available to that medium and appropriate to their stories.

But perhaps this proposal does not go far enough. Digital, online technologies present an opportunity to rethink the entire pedagogical process. Most Western universities, and their journalism programs still subscribe to very traditional models of teaching and learning. Knowledge areas are grouped into courses, ranging from "Introduction to Journalism," to "Basic" or "Advanced" "News writing and Reporting," to "Journalism Ethics." Courses take place during a 15- or 16-week-long semester, and students are graded or evaluated based on their performance. Is this really the best way for students to learn, with knowledge compartmentalized into narrowly defined modules? Would students learn better in an environment that integrated the specific tools and critical thinking fundamental to journalism into a seamless learning experience?

What if each day, week, or month led to the production of a news product, with every student having a turn to work in each newsroom role and on each aspect of the reporting, storytelling, design, editorial and management functions? What if ethics became a fundamental part of every decision rather than being relegated to a specialized niche?

What if diversity became part of every news decision instead of being considered only once during a Tuesday evening seminar? Could a

*Note: The author introduced this concept in his commentary for "News in the Digital Age," a conference report published by the Center for New Media at the Columbia Graduate School of Journalism, 1998 (www.cnm.columbia.edu).

school be organized so that every student was part of a central, news-gathering enterprise that produced stories using a range of media modalities? Instead of teachers working more or less on their own, could they work collaboratively to teach every student? Instead of students learning only during designated class hours, could they participate on a virtual 24/7 cycle using the asynchronous communications capabilities provided by online media?

Would this expand student learning? Would it be possible to identify the journalistic competencies (e.g., reporting, cross-media storytelling, ethics, etc.) all journalists should have and then evaluate students by measuring their mastery of these competencies? Is journalism education ready for its reinvention?

John V. Pavlik, Ph.D., is executive director of The Center for New Media, The Graduate School of Journalism, Columbia University, where he is also a professor.

chapter **3**

Way New Journalism Meets Lord Northcliff

News is something someone wants repressed.
Everything else is just advertising.
—Lord Northcliff

Online journalism must become the advance guard of the much-ballyhooed "New Media" of our age. It is bracing to re-call that the term "New Media" was used almost exactly 100 years ago, when Joseph Pulitzer was in his heyday making huge advertising profits from sensational stories and what was also called "Yellow Journalism."

This chapter explores the primary lessons learned over the more than 100 years of mass media U.S. journalism and how they can help journalists today avoid making the sorts of mistakes that have tarnished the news industry in the past. It also addresses the all-important business side of 21st-century on-line journalism.

■ Primary Issues in Reporting for Online Journalism

Wired, the Ladies Home Journal of the 1990s, has referred to traditional journalism as: "Monsters of the Old Media." Monsters they surely are. Yet, monsters, like dragons, are different depending on how you look at them. English dragons are nasty and wicked. Chinese dragons bring fortune and luck.

There is a mighty battle at hand among those who consider themselves the new media and what they regard as the old media. Expressed from the other point of view, there is conflict between real journalism and the pretenders to the throne.

Good dragon, bad dragon. This conflict, growing and shifting, is in fact a sign of great health, if also discord. It is precisely when the old is challenged by the new that great moments of creativity and insight often arise. This is an exciting time for journalism and for students of journalism, including not only those enrolled in university programs, but also those practicing the craft and those teaching it.

The challenges and changes presented by creating online journalism are akin to those that accompanied the creation of broadcast, the telegraph and the printing press. Some traditional considerations as well as some entirely novel ones are apparent right from the start.

True journalism is marked by key traits, much as a tiger is identifiable by its stripes, or a dragon by its fire. Among the traits necessary to real journalism are:

- Accuracy
- Attribution
- Multiple sourcing
- Fairness
- Thoroughness
- Freshness
- Originality
- Compassion
- Independence
- Relevancy

Although this list is by no means complete, it is a list that working journalists know is hard learned and hard kept. At the very least, any real reporter, editor or producer will agree that this list of traits is a solid beginning.

Journalists must be storytellers, and their stories must be of a high quality to meet the basic standards of the craft. In a multimedia environment the journalist faces an entirely new set of circumstances in trying to meet those basic standards that separate the trash from the treasure.

■ *Accuracy*

Journalist Seymour Hersch said, "The news is true. It is not the truth." In the traditional world of news, accuracy has meant getting the facts straight, such as how many people died on the plane, what the vote was in the legislature, and what was actually said. Journalists know they cannot explain the world, but they can help explain part of the greater context.

In the world of online journalism, none of that changes, but a major new player comes into the arena: the person reading, viewing and using the news and information. Because the barriers of participating in the story have all but tumbled away, the source can now add to the product that is presented as final, but in fact, never is.

Here's how it works. A reporter accurately reports that the legislature has voted 52 to 48 in favor of a bill mandating stringent new rules for airline safety, following the crash of a plane in which 123 people died. The author of the bill is quoted as saying that it is a victory; the leading opponent is quoted as saying that it will do nothing for safety but will increase costs for working people.

In creating an online story, the journalist must take advantage of the fact that the industry, the politicians and the people directly affected can have instant and universal access to the news site to add to the information. For example, they may shade their quotes differently or even change their votes after the publishing deadline.

This situation can be disconcerting for traditional reporters. Anyone with any experience knows that people will feel misunderstood, will change their minds, and will change their public positions to increase their advantage. In effect, the reporter loses a measure of control over the story.

The true point of this key change is that the standards for accurate reporting have suddenly become higher. Fulfilling this first commandment of journalism has suddenly become far more important and far more difficult than ever. And that's a very good thing.

■ *Attribution*

Real reporters have long gone out of their way to make sure their readers, viewers and listeners knew where the information came from because context is everything. If the airline industry provides numbers on safety, that's one thing; if an independent government inquiry provides these numbers, they're likely to carry more weight for most people; if colorful Uncle Cliff pulls them out of his hat, people will be more skeptical.

In an online news environment, attribution is more important than ever because the World Wide Web is filled with sites purporting to have authoritative information. Often, they offer misinformation. Often they ignore—or even disguise—the motives behind the data. The story about child labor in shoe factories might be on a site sponsored by a tennis shoe company. The story about the death of the rain forest may come from a Theodore Kaczynski (known in the press as the Unabomber). Too often the motives are unknown or the audience has not stopped to consider the source. Journalists do not have the luxury of being sloppy. Again, the standards are raised, and for the better.

■ *Multiple sourcing*

Multiple sourcing is a major issue in journalism and cannot be separated from attribution. The opposite of multiple sourcing is a single-source story. A story that has just one person, or source, is far more suspect than one with many sources, including people, documentation and data. In an online world, sources can be piled on with a simple link—and the temptation to do so is great, but it creates an entirely new set of dangers.

For instance, a story about Microsoft and Bill Gates could simply quote the Microsoft public relations people and their legions of enemies, or it could include links, allowing the reader to go to the Microsoft site, or to the Sun Microsystems site, or to anywhere else that would provide other sources.

Multiple links—multiple sources—are desirable. But there are some major issues. Journalists establish their credentials in part by having solid, commonsense, verifiable ways to separate the trash from the treasure and efficiently tell the audience what's real and what's not. That's a lot of what makes journalism valuable. Also, journalists know that linking out of a story is like changing the channel or putting down the newspaper. When the audience links out of a story, they may not come back to it. Journalists want people to read and see and use their stories, because they put a great deal of work, thought and (hopefully) soul into them. Further, they are more accurate, more fair and better contextually than are the primary sources individually.

A solution to these issues is to put all the links that matter at the *end* of the story on a separate source page, allowing the audience to see how the journalist used the multiple sources of information. Another solution is to link to what is called a "pop-up window."

For instance, should the story about Microsoft and Bill Gates include links in the story, allowing the audience to go to the Microsoft site or the (anti-Microsoft) Netscape site, or to anywhere else that would provide other sources? Taking this route is not a bad idea, because it would allow the audience to read, or hear, Gates or Netscape's Jim Barksdale speaking in their own words. The greater the number of relevant links, the better the information. They certainly don't have to be restricted to just the quotes or bites you used in your story. But there is a major qualification: Consider doing this only as long as the links taking the audience away from your site are at the *end* of your story, not *in* the story itself. Failing to do this may end with your audience leaving you and forgetting to return, a sin in journalism.

■ *Fairness*

This trait goes to the hard-to-define heart of the craft. What is fair? In the traditional world of journalism, journalists have been restricted by space and time to bringing forth representational sources of the story, providing a sort of north-south-east-west compass on the subject. They believe their readers and viewers and listeners understand that stories are thus sometimes incomplete, but fair. In an online journalism story, the limits are less confining. With links the journalist can create a bottomless well of facts, opinions, vantage points.

Would it be fair for a story about the Nazi genocide of the Jews, for example, to link to the frighteningly sophisticated Stormtrooper site on the Web, which advocates genocidal fascism? Or would creating that link be unfair because it gives weight to the worst of human failings? Because the true, fully mature and essential nature of journalism is one of inquiry, the question must be asked, knowing there may be no single correct answer.

■ *Thoroughness*

What multiple sourcing is to attribution, thoroughness is to fairness; one cannot be complete without the other. The limits so evident in

The World Wide Web makes everyone a potential publisher. The bad news is that people who have succumbed to humanity's failings, such as fascism, have a ready-made place to expose their problems before the world. The good news is that organizations that strive to keep the highest standards in journalism are now more accessible.

Used with the permission of FAIR (Fairness and Accuracy in Reporting).

print and broadcast are again blown to pieces by the Web. Because there are fewer corners in which to hide when creating online journalism, the challenges of providing a truly thorough story are even greater. There are, of course, limits on the journalist's time and on the amount of space on the server's hard drive, as well as limits to what editors and producers and publishers will allow.

It is imperative for online journalists to err on the side of too much, rather than just enough. Otherwise, they are failing to understand the medium and the challenge.

When providing suggested outside links for more information at the end of a story, approach it just as you would approach an annotated bibliography. You should visit the links you have posted to make sure you are not simply providing doors to virtual garbage cans in the name of being a thorough online journalist.

■ *Freshness*

News is like bread—it is best served fresh, and quickly goes stale. Although many stories do have a long shelf life, it is unfailingly useful to remember the root of the word *news—new.* For almost 200 years, this lesson has been a tested and true benchmark of journalism. When enterprising reporters rowed out into Boston Harbor to meet boats bringing news from Europe, they found it worked. When editors hired the first Pony Express riders to race information back to the newsrooms, they met with success. When a handful of farsighted publishers formed the beginning of the Associated Press to bring wire dispatches in from the front of the Mexican-American War, they found they could harness the speed of light and its power to accomplish a central aim of journalism.

There is far more to this idea than speed for speed's sake and beating the competition. The sense of urgency that comes with being first also contributes to lean, purposeful and aggressive reporting—all vital ingredients in exposing corruption, cruelty and avarice, or just finding great, interesting stories.

Online journalism provides perhaps the best arena for distributing news quickly. With transmission speeds of 186 thousand miles per second (the speed of electricity and light), journalists can directly connect millions of people. They can send words, pictures, sounds, and people can respond, add and subtract immediately. And they can do it anytime, around the clock.

The speed of delivering news has been increasing steadily since the rowboat. The Net has pushed it still further. Updated sports scores, presidential impeachments and stock prices may be sent directly to e-mail accounts, pagers and other emerging technologies. No longer do people have to wait minutes for a late edition or a broadcast break-in; they can be there live whenever they want.

The possibilities exhilarate and scare experienced journalists. The thrill of breaking a story is one of the most complete any reporter can have. Yet any seasoned journalist knows that haste brings the greatest risk of making a mistake.

There is, too, another huge battle taking place in journalism, as newspaper people argue the pros and cons of posting stories on the Web before they go to print. Does this take away the value of the paper? Or does it whet demand? Later this chapter will try to answer this question.

■ *Originality*

One of most maddening first fumbles of the Web is what has euphemistically been called "repurposed content." A more accurate and more popular term is *shovelware.* If true journalism is best served fresh, it also demands fresh ingredients.

The number of reporters in the United States is dwindling, even as the number of news outlets grows. Journalist Douglas Foster, former director of University of California at Berkeley's Graduate School of Journalism, found that the absolute number of newspaper reporters in the United States has declined significantly over recent years despite the rise in the population, or, more to the point, the audience. What these statistics indicate is a re-emergence of that oxymoron, old news. Here is an important message to all who have even the slightest interest in tomorrow: This growing habit of "repurposing content," is the equivalent of eating the seed corn.

News is not only new in time. Real news illuminates a previously darkened corner of the world. This takes real reporting, not a rehashing of stories already seen in a newspaper, a magazine or broadcast. The intrinsically fresh medium of the World Wide Web is especially conductive to originality. Great speeds, coupled with highly original and expansive storytelling potential, demand that if journalists are to realize the power of the Web they must invest in honest efforts to break news stories and draw an audience. A survey conducted in 1998 by Editor & Publisher found that the most profitable news sites were those "that develop original editorial content."

■ *Compassion*

Journalism has not been marked by compassion at every turn, and this lack of humanity is one reason journalism is in trouble. Journalism without heart is no more than a prosecutor's legal brief, a court reporter's transcript, a statistician's runs, hits and errors.

The stories that matter most to people, whether pseudocynical newsroom stereotypes like it or not, are the stories with soul. Real reporters know this because real reporters have done stories with heart and soul and have been startled by their audience's reactions. The true spirit of mature journalism is one of inquiry, not prosecution.

This is not to say that stories should be smarmy, pitiful tearjerkers or juvenile attempts to color reports with pathos. Rather, journalists should, in a disciplined way, allow the heart of the story to come out, not remain locked in a reporter's notebook.

Herein lies one of the great challenges of the Web. So far there have not been any truly excellent examples of capturing emotion online. This lack may be partially due to the fact that download times are far slower than the speed necessary to meet this challenge. But speeds are increasing fast and will soon allow journalists to use a full range of storytelling tools.

As New York Times former Managing Editor Gene Roberts told students at a San Francisco State University Future of Journalism conference several years ago, journalism is not dying, it's "committing suicide," in part because journalists have forgotten they are story-tellers, not scorekeepers.

■ *Independence*

Having a heart does not mean sacrificing brains. One of the many great touchstones of journalism is "Without Fear—Without Favor." Journalists have learned and relearned a hard lesson: When they embrace a cause, whether it is war, environmentalism, anticommunism or antibusiness, they are taking off their journalism armor and stepping into the costume of advocacy. Online journalists face special dangers, many as a direct result of the power to link. They must be especially careful not to use the power of multimedia, including hyperlinks, to tip the story to one side or the other.

There is a major exception to this rule: If you are purposely and openly reporting a story as an advocate—and there is some question as to whether that's ever appropriate in real journalism—then this power to tilt is yours to use. But if you choose to do this, be explicit and honest about your position and do not pretend to be objective.

■ *Relevancy*

Stories must be interesting or important and preferably both. If not, it isn't news. That's the essential starting point in news judgment. If the story you are considering is not relevant to your audience, why bother? The true challenge to the professional journalist is to make a seemingly irrelevant story come alive for the audience. For example, making stories about NAFTA (the North American Free Trade Agreement) relevant to many people was terrifically challenging, but the great storytellers got close.

Sometimes that type of experience prejudices news judgment. As an example, many editors later routinely buried stories about the

Journalists may report on fads, but those in the profession for the long haul are best advised to stay away from creating one to earn a living. Wired magazine began as an offline fad to talk about the online world, but its inattention to solid journalism contributed to its decline.

World Trade Organization. That is, until the group met in Seattle in 1999 and provoked street riots. It was then that many newsroom managers realized that the story was greatly relevant to many Americans and they had not played them high enough.

These guidelines have been a tried-and true standard for all successful journalism since the beginning. Online journalism is no different and in fact, may offer the best chance for recovering essential truths about the craft.

News organizations that forget these standards risk peril. Take Wired magazine as an example. In a few short years, Wired went from the darling of the Web community to the joke of the cognoscenti, largely because it couldn't find many of the basic values of news. So the discussion of values is back where it began, with the monsters of the old media versus the monsters of the new media. Be careful which dragons you send your knights out to slay—they may slay yours instead.

Basic Reporting

Online journalists are, first and foremost, journalists. They happen to work online. Journalists are charged with the responsibility of reporting the news, and even a quick glance at the 10 characteristics described in the previous section will make it clear that the job is not quite as easy as it may look.

It is helpful to have a basic idea of the standards to which all journalists must ascribe before taking on the significant challenges of applying these standards to the Web. For students beginning an online journalism production course, it is more helpful to have covered some basic beats than to know some basic coding.

The beat structure recommended for beginning journalism students consists of the basics from the most primary newspaper reporting:

- Business
- Courts
- Environment
- Investigative
- Local government
- Medical
- Police
- Politics
- Science
- Sports
- State and federal government

These areas represent the basic, old-fashioned beat structure, but do not cover everything. These beats often comprise subspecialties. For example, under the medical beat there may be an AIDS beat.

Large metropolitan newspapers often also have national and international beats and many specialized beats, including those covering issues particular to their communities (for example, the automobile industry in Detroit, the high-tech beat in the Silicon Valley, and so on). In addition, most decent newspapers have a feature and a sports section, and features and sports are very important to the Web.

The beat structure changes on the Web. The notion of community for a print newspaper generally refers to groups of people within the paper's circulation area. Since most newspapers still identify themselves with a city that has traditionally anchored a region (the Philadelphia Inquirer, for example, covers more than just urban Philadelphia; it also covers many of the suburban communities in the metropolitan area). In broadcast, stations define their community as the broadcast area, or ADI (Area of Dominant Influence), purposely trying *not* to restrict themselves to the old urban core.

On the Web, "community" has become a buzzword for several reasons. In the first place, there is far less emphasis on the geographic community because there are far fewer boundaries (if there are any at all). Instead, the communities on the Web tend to be groups of people with similar interests, regardless of where they live, work, or go to school. This situation has led to an inevitable boon for people selling advertising on the Web, which pushes the buzzword *community* even harder.

For example, say a person's interests are hip-hop music, ultimate Frisbee and early- to mid-20th-century American novelists, such as F. Scott Fitzgerald and Ernest Hemingway. Chances are this person is under 30 years old, has some college education, is physically active and has no children. This defines the community. People in the advertising industry, of course, know this. If this person's Web site, wherever it is based, has news and information of interest to this community, it will also attract advertisers of products designed for this population. Likely beats for this Web site might include Xtreme sports instead of baseball, alternative rock 'n' roll instead of easy-listening music, contemporary fiction instead of romance novels.

A good deal of thought and imagination will open up the possibilities, as they have at various publications. For example, the Orange County (California) Register has entertained the idea of a freeway beat, instead of simply a transportation beat. Communities with huge shopping centers have created mall beats. On the opposite side of the coin, less prosperous communities have created poverty beats. The Observer-Dispatch in Utica, New York, created a "Changing Economy, Changing Community" beat to deal with the massive changes taking place there after a military base and aerospace factory shut down and a casino opened up.

Some of the more imaginative beats are the "Not the News" beat, which covers stories that don't fit into any traditional category, such as a traditional **inverted pyramid** story about the sun rising. Gerald Grow at Florida A&M University points out that these kinds of stories allow people "to see with fresh eyes the things that have become disguised behind the routines of daily life." Mark Schleifstein of the New Orleans Times Picayune says his dream beat would be "trolling for stories at the New Orleans Convention Center. The mile-long convention center—yes, 5,280 feet long—results in New Orleans hosting literally hundreds of major conventions every year, all with interesting stories to tell." These sorts of imaginative, nontraditional beats are especially well suited to online journalism, whose audience is geared toward fresh approaches.

Once a beat starts to work, online journalists have an advantage that print and broadcast reporters have never fully enjoyed: the ability to have a great deal of direct participation by the audience. Early online Web site editors coming from traditional media were often a little shocked when they discovered this power to attract and hold people as well as to add depth and scope to their sites. For example, some editors expressed open amazement when members of their audience created their own *chat rooms* to talk about the O. J. Simpson trial and the coverage of the sensational courtroom drama. Soon afterward, online sites began creating special places for posting these sorts of dialogues for stories big and small. Audience participation not only helps identify the community, but also helps journalists keep track of what captures people's attention and what does not.

A fundamental familiarity with the basic beat structure is important to understanding and running a news site on the Web. Knowing one's way around these beats is sort of like knowing Java, JavaScript or Flash in multimedia production: It is a great bonus for college students immersing themselves in the future of news and information, but it is also an advanced step toward the mastery of the craft.

News features work particularly well for online university news sites. Such stories offer room to maneuver and if chosen well can stay relevant for substantial periods of time and present practical opportunities for trying different ideas. The extended time frame allows students to work on projects. In addition, as online sites will probably stay up and running for long periods of time, stories with what are called "long legs" will look fresher longer.

It is important to remember that the bread and butter of the news industry is breaking news. No online site should discard that significant piece without careful consideration. Breaking news is a vital and everyday concern among today's reporters, editors and producers working online. It presents major problems and opportunities, which will be discussed again in further detail later in this chapter.

By the beginning of 1999, online news had exploded from novelty status to a mainstay of news consumers according to a benchmark study conducted by the Pew Research Center for the People and the Press, based in Washington, D.C. The survey found that the number of American adults using the Web to get news and information zoomed from 23 to 41 percent in two years. People seeking mainstream breaking news and up-to-date weather information accounted for much of this increase. The survey also found that more than 80 percent of the people using the Web for news judged it largely as reliable as more traditional news media outlets—a trend that forecasts a bright future for online journalism.

Whether you are working on a long-term **evergreen** story, a **breaker,** or a Sunday **thumbsucker,** the basic standards of real journalism must apply. Otherwise, it's not news.

■ Retractions, Corrections, Clarifications

Take a look at page 2 of the New York Times on any day. It carries a standard feature: retractions, corrections and clarifications. The mighty Times is mighty, in part, because it knows that to be human is to make mistakes. And the principal value in making a mistake is to learn from it.

Good news organizations know this and do not shy away from the pain of retractions, corrections and clarifications. They embrace them because of the many opportunities they afford, among them:

- The accurate story is told and is told on the record.

- The reporter, editor or producer who made the mistake is more careful in the future because of public disclosure of the mistake.

- The publication declares its dedication to veracity and fidelity, greatly increasing its credibility and, therefore, its value.

Online journalism must make this same leap to reality and honesty to survive and prosper. Once again, though, there are special circumstances for this special medium.

If a newspaper makes a mistake in print, that mistake is forever on a piece of paper. The next day it might be on page 2 or somewhere else, but no one can go out and gather up all the papers from the day before and destroy them, as was so poignantly depicted in the film "Absence of Malice." Things are different in online journalism. The story can be altered on the server and all the people who view it afterward will see only what the publisher wishes them to see. On the face of it, this is a good thing.

On the other hand, this practice destroys much that is extremely important to the future of journalism. Unless the server has kept a copy of the original mistake—and few publishers will see the benefit of that—there will be no record of the original error. The sting of having made the mistake and having been publicly chastened, a mighty incentive for future accuracy, will be lost and along with it, much of the subtext of accountability for the publication. The credibility and value of the site and of online journalism will diminish.

A perfect case in point is an infamous story that ran in the San Jose Mercury News about an alleged tie between the CIA's reactionary tyranny in Central America and the sales of cocaine in the Los Angeles metropolitan area. The story received enormous play because Mercury Center—the newspaper's high-profile Web site—published the piece (http://www.sjmercury.com). If

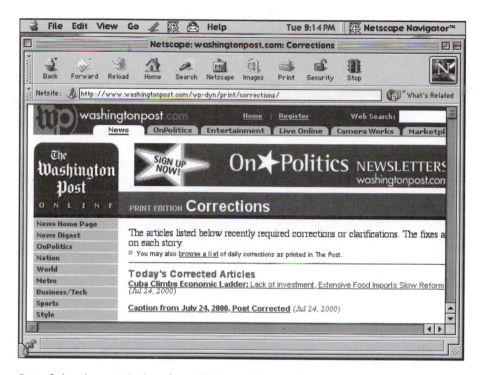

One of the characteristics of a solid journalism publication, online or off, is a regular location for corrections. The Washington Post's online site (http://www.washingtonpost.com) has a strong and relatively easy-to-find corrections section, shown in part here.

not for the Internet, not many outside the San Jose area would have noticed. But the Internet giveth and taketh away. The story was noticed because it was on the World Wide Web, and then it was torn apart by several of the nation's best and most credible newspapers. In response, the Mercury's editors quietly changed graphics in the online story that had implied incorrect information. Then, after a very long while, the story itself was pulled. Just disappeared. Just like Beria under Stalin. Eventually, there was a long retraction.

For real journalism to survive and prosper online, the site must have a place where retractions, corrections and clarifications can be easily found. Also, there must be an outright disclosure of the nature of a mistake because there is not likely to be another way to reference it. There is simply no comfortable way around this. There can be no excuse of running out of ink or space or time. Disclosure of errors is very much a primary issue in online journalism.

■ Traps and Triumphs in Partnerships

The World Wide Web is also a web of entangling alliances. And this model is now spilling over all the mass media. Online journalism offers great opportunities for breaking down walls and creating magnificent new enterprises.

For journalists who are constrained in doing their jobs by limits on time and money, alliances and partnerships are enticing—and they are typically sanctioned by business managers looking to save money and maximize resources in areas such as marketing.

The Chicago Tribune site, for example (http://chicago.digitalcity.com), has several partners, including the Lyric Opera of Chicago (http://www.lyricopera.com). What would happen if a scandal took place at the opera? Undoubtedly, a feisty, wealthy and storied paper like the Tribune would take it on. But what if the publication were a smaller, not so mighty and without a long history of battle? What if the partner were a consortium of local car dealerships and threatened to pull all its very lucrative ads from the site if the publication ran a story about a scandal involving the consortium?

In the Silicon Valley in the mid- to late 1990s, one major computer company offered many news and information sites special deals on its powerful new file servers, but did so under the guise of a partnership. Not only would the news site include advertisements for the computer company, but the news organization would use the company's software, which would make other competing—but useful—products incompatible. The choice for struggling organizations was difficult, but in the end the forward-thinking enterprises turned the computer company away.

Another option is to form alliances with other media organizations. These alliances, too, cause well-founded anxieties about independence and liabilities, but also bring opportunities to extend the reach and power of a Web site.

For example, a relatively small news site may lack the live traffic cameras that major broadcast outlets frequently control in large metropolitan areas. Having access to these cameras would almost certainly bring people to that site, especially in the mornings at their homes and in late afternoons, before and during the commute time, at their offices. But why would a TV station offer a link to its site to a small organization that lacks cash and clout? The smaller site must have something to offer. Perhaps it is a younger audience, which TV and print news outlets are losing to entertainment and, yes, the Web, or story ideas, or reporting, through internships or other innovative programs.

When an online site has intrigued and attracted a major media partner, potential dangers must be considered. If the larger partner is sued successfully for libel or fraud, will the smaller partner be named as a co-defendant? Will the managers of the larger partner insist on editorial control over some or all of the product? Will they use the online site as a way to take over the smaller partner's advertising accounts?

A common point of conflict arises in a situation that is less an alliance and more an internal sharing of power. Traditional news outlets such as newspapers and TV stations usually want—and now have—a Web site, but there is a good deal of discomfort and discussion about what exactly to do with this new beast.

The most common concern has to do with where to break news stories first: on the big money maker—the paper or the regularly scheduled broadcast—or on the Web? To online journalists the Web seems the natural answer because it allows the story to be posted quickly and it provides the audience universal and immediate access. In older newsrooms, this prospect can cause an uproar. The great worry is that the organization is scooping itself, and allowing its competitors to see what it has. These competitors can then get the stories ready for their paper editions and broadcasts.

Experience so far has shown that this fear is largely unfounded. According to Eric Meyer of the American Journalism Review site, NewsLink (http://www.NewsLink.org), the point made against posting on the Web is "a bogus argument." Meyer, who also teaches at the University of Illinois, says, "Virtually all research on the topic indicates expanded use of the printed product if the online product is treated as a promotional extension, which might include 24/7 updates" (*24/7* is shorthand for around the clock every day of the week). Meyer cites his own research on Tomorrow's News Today and work published in the Newspaper Research Journal.

In other words, getting its story first on the Web site tends to drive people to the main publication—or its partner. The opportunities and dangers are significant. But being a pioneer is always a risky as well as rewarding business. These are some primary issues in journalism that Lord

Northcliff didn't have to face. Nor did his friend and sometime partner Joseph Pulitzer, the "New Media" icon of his time 100 years ago. But today's journalists do.

■ Advertising

The press as it is known today did not really begin to emerge until the Industrial Revolution began creating factories that produced vast (and relatively cheap) quantities of shoes, tools and conveniences meant to be sold to the fast-growing populations of the 19th century.

How were the wonders of these new consumer goods conveyed to the buying public? Through newspapers, of course. How did these messages get in the newspapers? Through advertising.

The huge profits obtained by the first capitalists of the news industry—people like Bennett, Pulitzer and William Randolph Hearst—came from advertising, not from subscriptions. That business model has continued to define the success of capitalist journalism, including radio and television, in the United States. It will be the same for online journalism.

Because so much changes in the online world, online journalism sites face their own challenges regarding advertising. These challenges must be met to ensure survival because most news sites will not survive without advertising.

Much of the news in regard to advertising and online journalism is good; some is distressing. In 1999, just six years after the Web truly began to explode, a study by Editor & Publisher found that a surprising number

Joseph Pulitzer left a lasting journalism legacy through his annual prizes, but, in fact, made his fortune with sensational journalism, aggressive marketing and cutthroat business practices.

of news sites were already making money: "On average, media sites are reaching profit margins of 5 percent to 10 percent. Although many sites are experiencing margins in excess of 50 percent." In addition to the most important activity related to turning a profit, original news, Editor & Publisher also cited "savvy marketing" as a significant component of economic success.

Most professional journalists are rigorously trained to avoid any appearance of exchanging their professional integrity for advertising. Quality news outlets have fire walls between the advertising departments that drum up money to pay the bills and the news-gathering departments that are expected to report without fear or favor on everyone, including major or minor advertisers. This is how it must be if a journalistic enterprise is to be successful.

In the world of online journalism, the temptations for taking down the fire walls are new and powerful. Once down, however, a site's only real lasting marketing cachet—credibility—is destroyed and almost certainly cannot be repaired.

To begin with, there are the ubiquitous banner ads, the ads that typically appear across the top of Web pages. These ads are very often more flashy and dynamic than the news itself, creating an incentive for the audience to click on the ad and see more about the product. Rather than complain about this common situation, online journalists should pay attention to the elementary lesson before them: Make the news content at least as compelling, or more so, than the ads. Doing this takes an investment of time and money, but wise investments return large profits.

Other ads that have become common on the Web are sometimes called *stealth ads* by critics. These "advertisements" are in the form of links. An example would be a book review site that contains a link to a bookseller, such as Amazon, or Barnes & Noble or Borders, from which the book can be purchased. The bookseller typically returns some of the profit from each transaction to the original site—a mighty incentive, indeed, for including these sorts of links.

Fears about losing the audience to an entirely different site have been allayed in recent years by the increasingly common practice of having the link simply open another **window** in the browser, called a "pop-up window," leaving the main site visibly open just beneath it. This practice answers some objections, but it is still an uncomfortable development for professionals schooled in traditional journalism.

Delving a little deeper, another source of revenue, not necessarily related to advertising, is available to the online news publisher and makes

offline news owners envious. The Newspaper Association of America found in a 1999 study that 30 percent of people visiting online news sites have purchased merchandise or services online. People seeking profits (or just wanting to pay expenses without having to beg) in online journalism may want to consider more than a link to a bookseller. A story about late-model automobiles does not have to have a link to car dealers for price quotes, but there may be a place for such advertisements on the page where the story runs.

Real journalists know from historical example that there can never be a totally comfortable relationship between news and advertising, but that one's survival is often pegged to the other's, regardless of the medium involved. There are almost limitless possibilities in online journalism, from linking medical stories to cancer treatments, to linking garage-sale listings to classified ads. All require caution, thoughtfulness and honesty, for when you lose that, you will lose your professional standing, the standing of your colleagues, and the long-term viability of your news site and of other sites.

The Role of the Journalist as Both
Church and State in the New Media

DAVID WEIR

Traditionally, church-state discussions among journalists are framed in predictable terms: content is "good" and commercial concerns are "bad;" journalists are "ethical," whereas the ethics of their business colleagues are open to debate.

We are the church and they are the state.

The problem with framing the question this way with regard to the new media is that journalists are increasingly playing both roles at the same time. This is, after all, an equity culture. We are often part owners of the companies they work for and are simultaneously trying to produce honest journalism and help their new ventures succeed.

Because online journalism is a new medium we are inventing, we have an opportunity to establish new ways for the commercial side and the content side of their companies to work together. At this point, we do not want to believe that there is necessarily a contradiction between achieving the goals of building a successful business and preserving the integrity of content. We want to be optimistic about our chances of creating and implementing operational standards inside our companies that are consistent with the traditional values of journalism.

On the Web, people learn from one another about what does and does not work. Amazon.com, for example, has learned that it is not a good idea to call something a "recommendation" from its staff or its readers when it is in fact a paid (if undisclosed) advertisement. But the rules of the game are up for grabs, and that includes figuring out exactly what kind of business this is.

As Katherine Fulton of Global Business Network and others point out, news in and of itself is not a business. In the print and broadcast world, news is essentially the business of selling advertising, with lesser revenue streams from subscriptions and newsstand sales.

On the Web, content creation will not be a business until people start to pay for it. But unless a site has a monopoly over something people want, as local newspapers do with their archives, it cannot successfully charge for online subscriptions.

Currently, most online journalism sites rely on advertising revenue to pay their bills. This reliance brings the familiar pressures of the advertising world even more intimately into contact with content on the Web than in other media. In addition, advertisers today are often looking for the opportunity to develop "sponsored content". Instead of simply attracting ad banners to run on the content the site is already putting up, journalists and advertisers work together to create new content packages that the advertisers can support, or journalists "integrate" sponsored content within the existing site structure.

These kinds of deals suggest that a new business model is emerging. If so, who is better positioned to develop the business plan for a content company than the journalist?

What will be the essential characteristics of successful sites in a networked economy? In the age of interactivity and endless choices, where will people go for information? To sites that serve up hype or condescend to them by not disclosing their financial interest in their decisions? Or to sites they can trust and rely on?

If e-commerce is going to become ever more dominant on the Web, what is going to differentiate the sources of product information on e-commerce sites from one another? Who is going to insist on disclosure to the audience when a commercial relationship is determining the presentation of content? Amazon.com might want to pay close attention here.

Because journalists have long sought to connect with their audiences through getting the story right, they are the right people to determine the content strategies not only for media companies, but also for all the new entrants to the world of Internet publishing.

It is sometimes said that the Internet is turning everybody into a publisher. As these entrepreneurs with backgrounds in technology, finance, venture capital and various other disciplines discover the issues we have long been familiar with—how to establish trust with our audiences, how to achieve credibility, how to serve our audiences with accurate information in real time, and so on—they are finding that they have to turn to us for answers.

As for journalists, they need to learn the meaning of the new technologies, how to create successful business plans, how to be owners. This means they may have to break some old habits, such as being unwilling to breach the church-state line. They also need to know what habits *not* to break. They can ignore the fashionable conventional wisdom that content is dead. No community, and therefore no commerce, is possible online without honest content. No one goes online solely to visit Yahoo!, for example, or AOL. People go online to send e-mail, to do research, to buy things, to read Salon, to cite another example. Yahoo's role is like that of an airport in the offline world—people go there to get somewhere else. Content sites are the destinations people are seeking on the Web.

The key to the success of online journalism is the degree of control journalists are able to assert over the evolutionary process of building these content companies. Many new media companies are naturally run by people who do not come from journalistic backgrounds and who cannot be expected to automatically share the values, ethics, or instincts of journalists about establishing accuracy in the telling of stories.

Therefore, it is increasingly up to journalists to help figure out the business plan that will work for these new media companies. For those who find the prospect of working what is often called the dark side distasteful, remember what the great A. J. Liebling had to say about this question: "Freedom of the press is guaranteed only to those who own one."

Amen.

Photo by Marla Armuth.

David Weir is the vice president for network programming and editor-in-chief of Excite@Home. Weir is the former bureau chief and senior vice president, editorial operations, for Salon.com in Washington, D.C. He was previously managing editor and vice president of content development for Salon.com in San Francisco. He is a former vice president of content for Wired Digital (including Wired News and Hotwired); executive vice president of KQED, Inc., the fifth-largest public broadcasting company in the United States; acting news director for KQED-FM; editor of Rolling Stone, California, and Mother Jones; and editorial writer for the San Francisco Examiner. He was co-founder and executive director of the Center for Investigative Reporting, with clients including "60 Minutes" and "20/20."

Weir's books include "Circle of Poison," "Raising Hell," and "The Bhopal Syndrome." He has published over 150 articles.

He was an adjunct lecturer at the University of California Graduate School of Journalism for 14 years starting in 1985 and has won or shared over 30 journalism awards. As a screenwriter Weir worked on several film projects, receiving shared story credit for the Warner Brothers film "Rollover" with Jane Fonda.

chapter 4

Gathering Digital Data

I became a journalist to come as close
as possible to the heart of world.
—Henry Luce

The Internet is not only a remarkable way for journalists to dispense information, but it is also a significant new way for journalists to gather information. This chapter will consider some of the major possibilities and basic guidelines for gathering data online.

If possibility and danger have appeared to be growing themes so far, they will be still more evident here. This chapter takes the enthusiastic spirit of wanting to explore and understand the world and tempers it with the caution and intelligence needed to make the best of this new enterprise.

When Henry Luce, the founder of Time magazine, made his statement about why he became a journalist early in the last century, getting to the heart of the world was certainly as difficult a task as it is today. It required the tried and tested tools of great reporting: primary sources. That meant interviewing the people who actually made the story happen, finding the documents that proved it was real and then applying intelligence, discrimination and compassion to the mix.

None of that has changed for the journalists of the 21st century. What is different is that in the online world journalists are able to find so much more. But with the increased quantity of information comes the increased danger that a lot of what journalists are finding is bunk.

Most reputable newsrooms have full Internet access for all their reporters, editors and producers. The Internet is, after all, the largest encyclopedia, library, bookstore, university, phone book and reference section ever assembled. And it's all visible through the window of a computer monitor.

Information is the basic raw commodity of journalism. As rubber trees in Malaysia or Brazil are to tire manufacturers; as sugarcane and sugar beets in Cuba or California's Central Valley are to sugar companies; as raw oil in the Middle East or Alaska is to gasoline corporations, raw information is to journalism. Journalists take the raw material and refine it to rid it of impurities, alter its composition for use and package it for sale. Imagine an oil company's discovering a vast new supply of crude oil, some of it of questionable quality, but much of it top grade. That supply of crude oil is the equivalent of the Internet for people who gather information to be refined into journalism. Henry Luce would have been stunned. And perhaps troubled.

The Internet cannot always serve as a substitute for primary paper documents, working the phone or what some folks in the Silicon Valley call (tongue in cheek) "face mail" (face-to-face interviews). The Internet can help you get those documents, find those sources and discover a context. It can also result in an enormous amount of wasted time, several false starts and immeasurable heartache.

Despite the balancing act it demands, the Internet is beyond question the *sine qua non* for journalists of the 21st century. They simply must have it.

Essential Rules of the Game

The first thing you must have is a computer with full Internet access. Most universities today provide this access at little or no charge. This works well in some cases, but not so well in others. Where money is scarce, expertise is skimpy and the number of users overwhelms an anemic system this approach does not work well, and troubles are exacerbated if the school requires all students to have a computer and monitor.

An alternative to access provided by the school is access through a private ISP, or Internet Service Provider, such as AT&T, or through an online service, such as AOL. The customer signs up, pays the required fee (usually about $20 a month), and gets a password. Then the eager user gets an e-mail address and drives right on to the binary blacktop.

But, beware. Getting information on the Internet is simple—perhaps too simple. Terrible traps await on this Databahn. There are hoaxes, liars and just plain corrupt information—dirty data—a subject visited later in this chapter.

Let's say you are preparing a story about government pay and you want to find who are the top-paid government officials in your area. Your boss says, "Just get on the Web and download it. Have it to me by tonight's deadline."

You sign on the Net and go to one of your favorite reporter Web sites, say, The Reporter's Network (http://www.reporters.net/), Reporters Internet Guide (http://www.crl.com:80/~jshenry/rig.html) or A Journalist's Guide to the Internet (http://reporter.umd.edu/), and look for the search function. You type in "government pay," hit return and wait for the story magically to present itself. You might even be home for dinner.

Perhaps not.

First, there are no magic sites that have everything you want. If there were, all these stories would probably have been done long before. Second, access to that kind of information is fiercely protected by the people who stand to lose the most from revealing it. They make it hard to get to. And only very rarely would salaries be posted on the Internet. Although salaries of public officials are, of course, public information, getting access to them often requires a federal Freedom of Information Act request or the state equivalent (for example, the California Public Records Act). Third—and perhaps most important (this is called *burying the lead*)—even if the numbers were all there, how would you know they were accurate?

If your answer is, "It was on the government Web site," ask yourself, "Does the government ever make mistakes?" Is the data **refreshed** every day? Who **posted** the numbers on the site? Who has access to the server? You'll need answers to all these questions. Are you going to check the numbers with the personnel director and each listed employee?

AssignmentEditor.com is one of many excellent sites made specifically for journalists. It has dozens of excellent links to sites that help with everything from in-depth, investigative news to breaking stories. Like all good news and information sites, it has depth and speed and is continuously updated.

Used with the permission of the creator/CEO of AssignmentEditor.com. Copyright © 2000 by AssignmentEditor.com, Inc.

Perhaps this story is going to take a lot more work than you imagined.

Ironically, the Web has opened the doors to getting so much more information that journalists are increasingly pushed to do more, and that doesn't save time—it just creates huge new challenges.

Some basic rules for gathering information online can be immeasurably helpful:

■ Never *take for granted the authenticity or quality of information on the Web.*

Even if the database site is posted by credible organizations, such as Stanford University, The New York Times or your mother. Contact the people responsible for the site and check it. You—and they—have limited means to be sure the site is not phony, corrupted or sloppy. Attributing the information to the site doesn't necessarily protect you. In most states, you can be successfully sued for libel if you repeat attributed misinformation.

■ *Spend a serious amount of time getting familiar with some of the basic information available online.*
Bookmark and organize your basic sites and have them ready to go to in a pinch. For example, in California we are concerned with earthquakes, so the United States Geological Survey site (http://usgs.gov), along with several other key universities and commercial sites, is bookmarked in a folder called Earthquakes.

■ *Stay up to date on what is new and what is gone on the Web.*
That means investing a few hours every week keeping up. Things change significantly faster on the Web than in libraries and research institutes. In the Silicon Valley, time is often measured in dog years; one year on the Internet is the equivalent of seven years in the real world.

■ *Understand fully that there are limits on what can be done online and sometimes better and faster ways to get information.*
You can spend six hours finding out how many people died in the Chicago fire of 1871. And then you have to double-check it. Better to make a quick phone call to the Chicago Historical Society or local reference librarian. An inexpensive paperback almanac is always a quick and solid reference and often a much faster, more reliable source than the Web.

■ *Before you sign on, look at the clock.*
Write down what time you are starting your online research and what time you need to wrap it up. Stop at your deadline and look at your results. Was it worth the time and work for what you got? Have you reached a point of diminishing returns?

■ *Master, don't just learn, but master search engine techniques.*
You should be able to use the two basic types of Web search sites (Yahoo!, http://www.yahoo.com, and Google, http://www.google.com, are two good examples) and to construct efficient searches in all Web search machines. More on this later in this chapter.

■ *If you have a very speedy connection to the Net, such as a T-1 line or a cable modem, consider using a massive search engine, such as Metacrawler (http://www.metacrawler.com) or Dogpile (http://www.dogpile.com).*
These search most of the search engines for you. If you have a slower connection, such as 56K, you probably will want to restrict yourself to the standard search engines, such as Yahoo! or Google. Why? Because the time it will take versus the return is vital for journalists, who usually face demanding deadlines. Research shows that the standard search engines have access to little more than a fifth of the World Wide Web. But the big engines can take longer to download, even on a 56K modem.

■ *Some of the best research tools on the Web cost money.*
For reporters, sites such as KnowX, DJ Interactive and Lexis-Nexis can be exhilarating. Many of the pay-for-data sites are very affordable, just a few dollars for that key courthouse record from New Jersey, for example. Some will cost your newsroom hundreds, even thousands of dollars. And all may well be worth it. Take your time and investigate.

■ *Try using NewsLibrary (www.newslibrary.com) or NewsIndex (www. newsindex.com) for a free search of online newspaper archives.*
You may want to see what other newspapers have done with a specific story but don't have the money to use Lexis-Nexis or another pay-for-service search engine. These free search engines may not be as comprehensive, but they are a good start.

■ *Be very careful about taking what is often referred to as visual information (images, icons, pictures, etc.) off the World Wide Web and using it in your story.*
It is more often than not the property of the creator. The ease of borrowing images is spectacular on the Web, and this important topic is addressed in greater depth in Chapter 9. For now, consider taking images off the Web the equivalent of hopping in a car left running with the keys in the ignition and taking it for a spin around the block—that's grand theft auto.

■ *Remember that the World Wide Web is, after e-mail, the most used part of the Internet, but it is just one part.*
If you say you've searched the Net and you have really searched just some of the Web, you may be misstating the facts.

There are some basic rules of the road governing the use of Web sites for reliable information. The heart of the matter is knowing what is credible, useful information and how it can be used. First, know whether the site you are looking at is credible. The questions that follow have direct application to your story or site as well. If you are using them to judge the worthiness of the information you seek, you must expect others to be able to judge you the same way.

- *What person or organization is behind the site?*
  Look carefully at the Web address. Does it end in .com, .gov, .org, .net or .edu? The White House site, for example, ends in .gov. There is also one that ends in .com, but it's a pornographic site.

- *Does the Web address include a tilde (~)?*
  This is often an indicator that it is an individual's personal home page. This is okay, as long as the site is not suggesting it is more than that and as long as that's what you are looking for.

- *When was the site last updated?*
  This information may be readily available on the site itself. If not, there are other ways to find it. The Netscape Navigator browser, for example, allows you to click the View menu at the top and go to Page Info, which sometimes provides the last true revision date.

- *Is the site filled with misspellings and syntactical errors?*
  If so, look out. That's a sign of poor workmanship and lack of reliability.

- *Who is behind the site?*
  You can get this information by using the "whois" function on http://rs.internic.net or by going to http://www.checkdomain.com, which is easier to remember. Some people recommend using a software tool, called Alexa, which is free and available at http://www.alexa.com, for tracing information. There are privacy concerns, however, as Alexa tracks every online move you make after you install it.

Searching for people behind the sites has other uses besides ascertaining their legitimacy and the reliability of the information. If you wanted to reveal the people in your community behind a child pornography site, for example, this would be a good place to start.

Using Search Engines

Because search engines will probably figure prominently in your quest for information, you need to take the time learning to use them wisely.

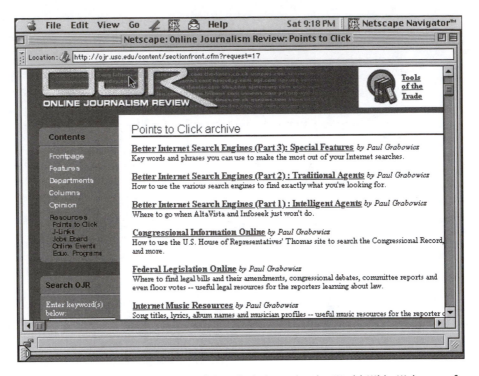

Search engines such as Yahoo! and Google help make the World Wide Web one of the most useful and revolutionary tools in the history of mass communications. Paul Grabowicz, a professor at the U.C. Berkeley Graduate School of Journalism, writes regularly in the Online Journalism Review with excellent tips and updates about making search engines work for you.

Used with the permission of Online Journalism Review.

There are two basic sorts of search engines. Yahoo! (http://www. yahoo.com) and Google (http://www.google.com) will serve as the two examples here.

Yahoo! is a good example of what some people call a hierarchical engine. (Some others argue that Yahoo! is not a search engine at all, but a *directory*. Find two people who know something about the Web, and you will find an argument about something.) Let's say you want to find out about Finnish bolts exported to New Zealand for use in washing machines. You start with Business and work your way down (more Silicon Valley jargon: *drill down*) until you find what you are looking for.

Google is a good example of a nonhierarchical search engine. You start with a reasonably sophisticated search for what you want and hope it takes you there or close to it. Search engines are always trying to make their services easier to use—and that requires that their users keep up with their search techniques. Find at least two you like and stay sharp on their search techniques.

There are some elementary rules for effective and efficient searches:

■ *Think for more than a moment about what you really want.*
If you want to know how many bolts were made in Finland last year, that's different from wanting to know where those bolts went or what they were used for. Your search will differ depending on your goal.

■ *Learn Boolean logic.*
It may sound like bad writing from "Star Trek," but there is such a thing and it works for you on the Web. Named after the 19th-century English mathematician George Boole, Boolean logic has four basic commands: AND, OR, NOT and NEAR. You type AND in your search when you want both words or quoted phrases to show up in the results. "Finnish bolts" AND "New Zealand dams." You use OR when your search is a little more liberal. "Finnish bolts" OR "bolts from Finland." You use NOT when you want to exclude information. "Finnish bolts" NOT "cloth" NOT "finish."

■ *Use advanced search functions frequently.*
Especially when you are looking for anything more than the obvious, using advanced functions will not only speed up your work, but will keep you sharp on the techniques of your favorite Web search engines.

■ *Focus your search so precisely that your first results will be 0 found.*
Then you can shed some of your precision and cast your net a little wider.

■ *If your search results are extensive, stop and refine the search further.*
Don't run through the first ten pages of your results. Most browsers have a find function that allows you to type in a word or phrase. It's sort of a search within a search. For example, an AltaVista search for Finnish bolts dredged up 196,000 documents. Using the find function and typing in "export" and "United States" will narrow the

search to the documents among the 196,000 that use those words and phrases.

■ *Use quotes around the phrases you are looking for and try to use as many phrases as possible in each search.*
Let's say you are now interested in bolts from Finland used to make dams in New Zealand under the consultation of the U.S. Army Corps of Engineers. You would search for "Finnish bolts" AND "New Zealand dams" AND "U.S. Army Corps of Engineers."

■ *Make sure the search is not case sensitive.*
If you use a case-sensitive search for "Finnish bolts," for example, you might miss sites that failed to capitalize *Finnish.* More likely, you'll miss out on sites that did capitalize *bolts.*

■ *Use shortcuts and tricks that work on the Web.*
For example, if you are looking for a photo of Walter Cronkite, type "Walter Cronkite" and "jpg" because photos of the former CBS anchorman are most probably in a jpg format. The asterisk (*) can give a little wiggle room for misspellings or derivations of words. If you are looking for someone whose last name is Anderson, but you don't know whether it is spelled "sen" or "son," a search for "Anders*n" may be the way to go. A favorite trick of journalists is to type "link" in a search. The most famous example occurred when the Heaven's Gate cult committed mass suicide. Reporters got on the Web, went directly to their favorite search sites, typed "link:heavensgate" and found not only the Heaven's Gate site but other cults that linked to it.

Most of the time when *gathering* information journalists use the Internet to gather information that has already been printed, broadcast or posted. Typically, online journalists use the Web much as print reporters use newspaper clippings from the library (or what the real old duffers used to call the morgue) or broadcast people use old scripts and file tapes. Journalists want to see what has already been published or aired because they know and fully understand a very basic, fundamental principle of journalism: *News is new.* Journalists want fresh material. Serving up a story that has already been around is like serving old fish to guests. They probably won't want to come back.

If you are gathering off the Web only information that has already been posted as news, you are scraping refried beans off someone's plate and serving them to another person as a new dish. You are not a news-person. If you are working for someone who does not understand the ultimately suicidal nature of delivering this kind of "news," look for another job.

Computer-Assisted Reporting

The most notable use of the computer for reporting is what the pros call CAR—Computer-Assisted Reporting. The National Institute of Computer Assisted Reporting, or NICAR, (http://www.nicar.org) holds an annual convention in the United States as well as many smaller, regional conventions across North America. These provide wonderful opportunities to get involved and comfortable with such disturbing terms as *parsing, relational databases* and *record layout miscues.* Like so many other technical tasks, computer-assisted reporting can be complicated and intimidating to beginners. But for students of introductory online journalism, there is no need for such fear. Some of the most essential tools are easily obtainable and make it possible to think through, pursue and ultimately report stories that were all but unapproachable by journalists just a generation back.

Some of the basics:

- *Spreadsheets*
  Virtually every word processing system contains spreadsheets. Perhaps the best known is Microsoft's Excel, usually **bundled** with Microsoft's ubiquitous Word program in its widely used Office suite of software. The spreadsheet, formerly the province of bookkeepers, is a fascinatingly elegant way to collect data and see in a glance where a story is going. For example, a journalist might collect data on travel expenses of local politicians and line them up in columns that would quickly show who was spending the most over any specified amount of time.

- *Databases*
  Spreadsheets with attitude. After learning some basic database managing techniques, you can find a great quantity of raw numbers right on the Internet and drop them into a master spreadsheet. A database program can run through the numbers in seconds, organize them and summarize the findings with breathtaking speed. For example, a journalist could take the raw data of travel expenses (assuming they were

available in a digital form and thus able to be dropped into a program) of a variety of politicians and make vast comparisons in no time.

■ *Relational databases*
Attitude combined with brains. Two or more databases can be mixed together to form a relational database. To continue the previous example, the travel expenses could be mixed with a database detailing salaries or offices. The journalist could then see if the best-paid office holders were also those who traveled most, or if members of Congress were more prone than governors to spend taxpayers' dollars on travel.

A major concern with computer-assisted reporting is dirty data. Numbers from any source can be sullied, improperly placed and downright wrong. Once the data have been acquired, you must go back to the source and verify their accuracy. Look for any obvious or troubling inconsistencies, which may prove to be either the most important part of the story or a mistake. Nothing should be taken on faith. Or, as an old news hand once pronounced the first rule of journalism, "If they can move their lips, they're lying."

Acquiring, using and ultimately relying on raw data as a foundation for journalism has become, in large part because of the Internet, a specialty unto itself. And a vital one. But it is important to remember that delivering data is *not* reporting—it is only a part of it.

A minor revolt is brewing among serious journalists about the phrase "Computer-Assisted Reporting." According to Phil Meyer, teaching at the University of North Carolina at Chapel Hill, "CAR is an embarrassing reminder that we are entering the 21st century as the only profession in which computer users feel the need to call attention to themselves." In a piece for the Poynter Institute Meyer wrote: "Journalism today is in a battle for survival against the forces that would merge it with entertainment, advertising and public relations. What practitioners of CAR have been after—whether consciously or not—is a higher standard of truthtelling. . . . A computer is helpful in doing that. But the computer itself is not the goal, nor does it define what we are trying to do." These wise words should also give journalists pause about their love affair with the computer for disseminating, in addition to collecting, news, and deserves their full attention.

Regardless of language, terminology or definitions, computer-assisted reporting has much to do with the Internet. Because of it, journalists are able to perform simple functions such as sending e-mail, find expert sources online and get data for spreadsheets and databases. All the numbers, facts and raw data in the world can be found and presented to readers, but real reporters must never lose sight of their mission as society's storytellers—who tell true stories.

■ E-Mail, Newsgroups and Mailing Lists

The most elementary and perhaps most important tool is **e-mail.** Through it, journalists are able to communicate quickly and efficiently with many people, even sending video, audio and book manuscripts. They can also abuse it.

There is a phenomenon similar to road rage on the Net. Some people feel perfectly free to insult, denigrate and simply hurt others with messages. They feel shielded from responsibility. Young journalists seem prone to this as much as any group, sometimes getting angry at sources, or potential sources, for not providing desired information. Journalists should guard against this tendency. Not only is **flaming** in bad taste, but all messages are recorded somewhere and thus may be used against their senders later, possibly in court.

E-mail interviews deserve some special thought and consideration. A well-done examination in Editor & Publisher's excellent online site (http://www.mediainfo.com) pointed out that "electronic mail has quickly become a powerful, compelling newsroom aid. Among other things, it smooths communications with both the public relations community and general public. At the same time, its place in the newsgathering process has yet to be clearly defined."

Some of the great benefits of e-mail interviews also include having a written record of the source's responses, fast and affordable ways to communicate across great distances and a businesslike efficiency that takes away the sometimes false coloring of personalities. But there are dangers. The main one is basic: How does the journalist know the true identity of the respondent? There are services that allow people to cloak their true names.

Online journalist John C. Dvorak says he has corresponded with Microsoft's Bill Gates and knows his personal writing style—but warns he never uses the quotes or information unless he independently verifies them. Some people, Dvorak says, "can make it [the e-mail] look like it comes from the Microsoft server."

Gerry Yandel of the Atlanta Constitution has greater reservations. "E-mail is inadequate" he declares, "especially for news writing." Yandel, like many experienced street reporters, points out there are hard-to-quantify but disturbing questions about e-mail interviews. Really good journalists are often better than average at sensing a lie or a source with little credibility. They usually pick up signals because they are extremely sensitive to the inflection of a voice, a pause, a glance. The further away the journalist is from the primary source, the further away the journalist is from using these senses—and thus from getting the real story.

Print reporters who have moved to broadcast will eagerly testify to the barrier put between them and their sources with a $50,000 TV **beta-cam** and **stick microphone.** E-mail is another such barrier that allows—some might say encourages—a source from revealing the true nature of a story.

Inviting the audience to comment on stories, provide news tips and otherwise make direct contact with reporters is a great step forward for both sides of the fence, but like so many new aspects of journalism, needs to be approached with caution.

A useful collection of e-mail is found in what many people refer to simply as chatrooms or message boards—in the past more commonly called a BBS, short for a bulletin board service. People can post messages online in a variety of loosely organized forums, read what others have posted and—beware—get a skewed idea of a topic. Let's say you are doing a story about presidents who have trouble distinguishing truth from lies. You might seek a BBS for people with a serious interest in history and presidential prevaricating. But don't forget, if you post a message on the Internet, it may stay there for many, many years. Be careful.

Similar forums called **newsgroups,** can be found on a portion of the Internet called **Usenet.** A newsgroup is an e-mail-based network where, in

The microphone has long been the concern of only broadcast journalists, but in the online world that distinction will vanish. Older microphones are now collector's items, but the newer instruments used to record audio are already becoming standard issue for the online reporter.

addition to mere chatting, you may also find people and organizations (often companies) selling an idea for fun and profit.

The term *newsgroup* may imply something to do with news, and sometimes people refer to the postings in newsgroups as "articles," further confusing matters. But newsgroups are about whatever they want to be about. The most infamous are the ones with the alt.sex address.

Sites such as http://www.deja.com and http://www.supernews.com/ are sources for newsgroups that deal with such topics as journalism. There is an alt.journalism forum and there is an alt.journalism students' place on the Internet.

The purpose of these adventures for real reporters is usually to find sources. Many sites on the Web itself will provide links with sources in public relations, academia and industry. ProfNet (http://www.profnet.com) is one of the more popular sites. Others include NewsPlace for News and Sources (http://www.niu.edu/newsplace) and Sources and Experts (http://sunsite.unc.edu/slanews/internet/experts.html).

Mailing lists are a wonderful, horrible, fascinating, droning, time-saving, time-wasting way to get information on anything, everything and nothing of value. Confused? Here's the story: The most popular electronic lists are called Listservs, a trademarked name that comes from a software program developed in 1986 that makes it easy to post e-mail to a group of subscribers. Others are Listproc and Majordomo. These lists are, essentially, groups of people online who communicate with one another through e-mail. There are well over 100,000 such lists.

You might want to subscribe to a Listserv that deals specifically with online journalism. From then on, you will get e-mail sent to everyone who has subscribed. Much of it is banal (someone from New York posts a message asking if anyone knows any good Web sites for lost pets), some of it is excellent (someone from Los Angeles posts an obscure Web address of a coding genius in Costa Rica that prompts a discussion online about why journalism sites can't be that interesting and well done). If the list isn't useful a simple e-mail message is all it takes to unsubscribe.

There are Listservs for almost anything. If you are toying with the idea of doing a story about overweight Americans, you can join several Listservs devoted to discussing related issues, enabling you to read what's on some people's minds and even getting access to excellent sources who may have escaped attention otherwise. You can also get burned. It is not uncommon for a reporter to pick up bad leads, false tips and generally bad sources through mailing lists. If you have all the time in the world and have no life, getting dozens, even hundreds of e-mail messages each day through these lists can be nice, probably. But if you are like most busy people, you may find they can clog up your e-mail inbox and drive you crazy.

A final caution: *Never* open attachments sent to you unsolicited or from sources you do not know. Attachments are a favorite way to send viruses across the Internet, and simply opening one can erase your files, damage your software and cause immeasurable headaches. Unsolicited attachments, whether from public relations firms, e-mail lists or anywhere else, should be trashed immediately without being opened.

■ Digitized Photography and Sound

In a multimedia world, journalists are not content simply to do a telephone interview and jot down a few notes and quotes. The challenges are greater. *Visual information* is a key phrase. Though barely evident on the Web today, digital photography will open amazing new vistas.

Many, many photographic images are already on the Web, and many of these can legally be used. What was once the domain of the newspaper graphic artists as **clip art,** is now online, sometimes called **click art,** and is available to anyone who wants it. Copying an image in the **public domain,** say, a photo of George Washington, is as easy as several clicks of the mouse. But real journalists are also vitally interested in creating their own original content.

Digital cameras have one great benefit: Images can be taken directly from the camera and dropped (**ported**) into the computer to be used in a story. They also have one great disadvantage: The images do not have the deep resolutions—quality—of the images from film and video cameras. That will change, and journalists should be familiar with digital technology.

There are two types of digital cameras: One uses a CCD technology, and one uses CMOS (pronounced "sea-moss") chips. The CMOS technology appears to be headed for the finish line first; it is less expensive and produces better-quality images. Oddly, digital video cameras are ahead of the still machines. The image produced by these cameras can be nearly as good as those produced by the best $50,000 professional video cameras; the sound is at least as good, and sometimes better. Digital motion cameras are also remarkably small. Not only are they easier to cart around than are traditional TV cameras, but they also interfere less with getting the story.

For journalists in the 21st century, understanding video will be critical. The time is fast approaching when **real-time video** will be available to everyone on the Web—that means every second 30 frames will download, just as they do on television. Now, **compressed video** delivers about half that—15 frames per second. But at that rate the video takes so long to get to the viewer that current uses of video online are little more than experimental.

In the next five or 10 years, as real-time video spreads through the Web, the wall between the Web and TV will crumble and disappear. Aside from a small niche of print writers, tomorrow's journalists will be able to use powerful storytelling tools once restricted to people working in TV. This *convergence* is likely to change most everything journalists think they understand about mass media.

For example, imagine a sports program covering a football game. Viewers at home leave the room just as a crucial play begins. They return to find it is over. Today they are at the mercy of the station or network, which will probably show a replay. But with technology that is already available, any part of the game can be replayed without having to rewind tape. In the near future, in addition to seeing that play over and over, viewers are likely to be able to compare it with other, similar plays in other games. Or they will be able to see a referee's calls made throughout the season. Viewers will be able to bring their perspectives to the game and use video to make a point. All this activity may be moderated and used by the sports reporter of the future.

This is not to say that still photography will die. There is much power in the captured moment. Photography means "writing with light," and none of us can ignore its power. The next chapter will return to this subject.

The power of sound is less obvious but arguably more intimidating. Digital audio recorders are readily available, their prices already well within range of most organizations and their quality excellent. After being captured on a hard drive, however small, audio can go directly into the computer, where the sound can be used in a story to great effect—and at great peril. As with visual graphics on the Web, it is easy to copy audio online, and **sound files** are often legally usable.

For example, the opening page of our news site NewsPort, (http://www.NewsPort.sfsu.edu) has often used a ship's horn taken from a CD of sounds in the public domain. But to use an actual interview with a source in a story, it must be recorded and dumped into the computer and then the journalist must decide where and how to use it in the news story. The next chapter will deal with these issues.

Musings on the Future of Journalism

MARK POTTS

Imagine a world with no newspapers. *bah!*
It may be coming sooner than you think. Cast aside the idea of ink on paper; indeed, think beyond the notion of words on a computer screen. News and information in the future will be available through means now almost unimaginable, in forms we're only beginning to comprehend.

It's easy to look at the dramatic changes wrought by the Internet in the past few years and think that we're already seeing the future of journalism—one that involves greater immediacy, more personalization, increased reader participation and bottomless depths of information. But that's like looking at television in the 1950s and envisioning that medium forever consisting of only black-and-white renditions of corny situation comedies starring old radio personalities.

The newspaper you carry under your arm today and read on the bus or subway is going to metamorphose—to pick one vision of the future—into a light, thin computer page that's just as portable as its printed ancestor. On it you'll be able to watch—not read—a story that is told through a combination of text, video and 3-D animation and simulations and customized to your liking. Want to learn more? It's just a (wireless) click away. Disagree with the point of the story? Summon the reporter (or news maker) to the screen and argue with her. Want to know what other readers think? Their opinions are at your fingertips—and so is your ability to put in your two cents. Want to buy a product described in the story? Order it right off your screen. Need to get off at the next stop? Roll up the screen and stick it in your pocket. You don't even get any ink on your hands.

It sounds like something out of "The Jetsons," but it's hardly science fiction—most of the technology and know-how for such a product is in the laboratory right now. And that's just a taste. New types of devices, high-speed wireless connections, supercomputer-like speed and many other advances are going to change significantly the way we get, use and interact with our news and information, not to mention the way the media business deals with its audience and earns its money.

What does such a futuristic world mean for the craft of journalism? The good news is that a lot of the basics won't change. There still will be a premium on credibility, objectivity, accuracy and fairness. And it's hard to see those old standbys who, what, where, when, why and how becoming extinct.

But many other elements of the profession are going to be very different. We've already seen the emphasis that the new media have put on speed. In an ever-faster, more competitive world, the pressure to be first with a story is hardly going to abate. That will require new diligence about getting things right before releasing news and information to the world in these fantastic new ways.

At the same time, we're going to be able to explore and exploit entirely new forms of storytelling. Today journalists tend to think in terms of a single, primary medium, such as text or video, occasionally augmented by the token grainy photo or superimposed graphic. But the new devices will hardly know such bounds. Some stories will lend themselves better to video, augmented by text archives or documents; others might work better through a combination of short text pieces illuminated by video and audio; still others might best be told by making the reader a participant in a simulation to experience things directly.

We also need to get used to a basic change in their relationship with the audience. It's no longer strictly a one-way street. Publishing, by its nature, implies pushing information out to the masses; the new media, by their nature, allow a two-way connection—that new cliché of interactivity. Readers and viewers will be able to talk back—and they'll expect a response. Members of the audience will be allowed to share opinions and experiences with their peers, absent the journalist's traditional role as gatekeeper in what some have called participatory journalism.

We can't consider the future of journalism without also taking a close look at how the business of journalism is going to change. The longtime financial underpinnings of the news business are being challenged dramatically by the new media.

Consider the classifieds, which have been an economic bedrock of the newspaper business for generations, providing as much as 50 percent of newspaper revenue. The new computerized media greatly enhance classifieds, allowing them to be searched and customized. That makes printed classifieds an anachronism.

Newspapers that for years had job, home and merchandise listings all to themselves now face stiff competition from hundreds of upstarts armed with better technology and more focused business plans. Similarly, new forms of retailing, new intermediaries in the business-to-business marketplace, even new types of news and information services are pecking away at the hegemony long enjoyed by traditional news media. The results, in a few short years, are likely to be catastrophic for traditional news companies unable to adapt.

The corporate survivors of this revolution will be those companies that can change along with the markets and the technology, those that can fit their business models to the new reality and find ways of extracting money through e-commerce and business services rather than through advertising and subscriptions. Many of these mutations will put new sorts of pressures on the old walls between church and state in media companies, walls that will need to be thoughtfully defended for the sake of credibility.

In the years to come, all these changes—and more still unimagined—are going to churn through journalism. Time-honored brand names and media types will wither and die; new ones will rise up to take their place, creating fresh opportunities. The best journalism requires a good deal of flexibility, and journalists will have to employ that same sort of agility in dealing with the changes around them.

As you adjust to and take advantage of this revolution, take a step back and be sure to realize something remarkable: This cataclysmic change occurring in the journalism profession may be the most exciting story you'll ever get to see up close.

Mark Potts has been a longtime editor and reporter for The Washington Post, Chicago Tribune and San Francisco Examiner. He was also a co-founder of Washington Post. Newsweek Interactive. He is currently vice president and chief product officer for the Internet division of Cahners Business Information, the nation's largest trade magazine publisher.

chapter 5

A Message for Each Medium

The electric technology is within the gates,
and we are numb, deaf, blind, and mute about
its encounter with the Gutenberg technology.
—Marshall McLuhan

In assembling the parts of an online story the journalist must consider what role each part plays. Journalists often think of themselves first and foremost as writers. Writing for an online environment raises its own issues, which this chapter will explore in some depth.

Powerful new storytelling tools are available today. Video, audio, graphics and interactivity are all now part of the palette, as journalists paint their stories, and online news sites. This chapter offers a look around the new supply store that online journalism has opened.

■ Writing for the Web

When all is said and done about the wonders of the World Wide Web, multimedia online is still very much in its infancy. Despite its multimedia video streaming, **real-time audio** and **animated GIFs,** the reality is that the principal medium online remains the written word. It is mightily augmented in the best sites by **visual** and **audio information,** but strip away the few pictures and graphics and you will see words—many, many words—on the Web.

This is a little sad, but understandable. Journalism has not yet caught up to the technology. What is harder to understand is the lack of attention to how writing for an online world is vastly different from writing for the printed page. Journalists cannot afford to ignore these differences, as writing is their principal means of storytelling.

The first concern is how people read on the Web. Simply put, readers are staring into a light bulb with letters written across the glass. Not the optimal circumstances for great storytelling. Resolutions of the printed word on the screen are weak, and the light is irritating after a while. Although vast improvements are promised in the near future, it will certainly be several years before masses of Web users get better depth and clarity.

Try this little test of your own to see how it works: Write a few hundred words on your computer without using the spell, style or grammar check functions on your word processing program. When you are done, edit on the screen. Fix every mistake you see. Now print your copy and proofread again. You will most certainly find more errors. How could you miss those obvious mistakes? Easy. On paper, the letters are dark and deep with magnificent resolutions. And the only light is reflected off the paper, not coming from the other side.

On a few sites this situation is clearly understood—one prize-winning photostory posted several years ago by Mercury Center (http://www.sjmercury.com) even exploited the light-behind-the-photo phenomenon—but examples of good Web writing are rare, indeed.

Author Martha Sammons points out in her "Internet Writer's Book" that "reading is slower online: reading speed decreases by about 30 percent." Readers become frustrated with this situation and lose interest. Online journalists need to remember that they are pioneers working in a revolutionary medium so that they don't get frustrated as well.

The first Bibles printed with a Gutenberg press were called debasements of the soul, having nothing written by a hand guided by God. Painters similarly denounced the first photographs. Television news, still very much a young medium (and surely to be seen one day as training wheels for news and information on the Web), remains widely considered a heresy by those truly familiar with only print journalism. Prepare to be considered a heretic yourself, as you become a pioneer 21st century journalist.

It is important to keep in mind the following considerations when writing online:

- *People do not read carefully online.*
  They scan. The inherent and immediate discomfort with reading on a monitor means that people scan for what they are looking for. If it takes too long to find what they want, they leave.

- *"Too long" is a matter of seconds, not of minutes or of word counts.*
  Commercial Web site managers consider it a victory when a person stays on any site longer than a few minutes. The chance that a reader will stay on a story or even on the first page of a story for more than 60 seconds are remote. It's not the story, it's the medium. At a recent Internet convention called Beyond the Banner, researchers presented evidence that the average stay on a popular search engine such as Excite (http://www.excite.com) is 1 minute, 30 seconds. The average stay at the Boston Globe's Web site (http://www.boston.com) is almost 11 minutes. That's better news for advertisers and investors in online news sites, but it's still not great.

- *The remote control is essentially the same as a computer mouse or tracking ball.*
  The television has trained us all how to use the screen. Unless people are captured quickly and held tightly by the story line, they will move on fast. Television executives fully understand that theirs may be the only products in the marketplace (with the possible exception of radio) for which consumers make purchasing decisions (deciding what program to watch) in their own homes and offices simply by pushing a button at their fingertips. This is exactly the same model as the Web.

- *People come to the Web for information.*
  This is good news for anyone in the news industry, and journalists are in an excellent position to make use of it. Getting information must be a quick, pleasant and useful task. Ancient lessons on storytelling coupled with the reliable facts that make up the journalist's craft are perfectly suited to the online world.

■ *Bulleted lists and other clear graphic elements are essential to successful online writing.*
They allow readers to get the information they want quickly. Long narrative writing, on the other hand, is not well suited to the Web.

■ *Writing in brief, bright bursts of light works best.*
Writing on the Web means using spare, well-chosen, carefully crafted prose. There is an old story about a person who wrote a terribly long letter to a friend. The writer apologizes at the end for its length, saying, "I would have written a much shorter letter, but I did not have the time." This lesson is particularly important for writing online.

■ *People prefer inspired e-mail.*
Almost everyone has had the unpleasant experience of opening an e-mail message and seeing hundreds of words, so many that to read them all will require scrolling down past the end of the screen. And almost everyone prefers quick, snappy and clever e-mail. That's the model for online writing.

■ *Visuals need to be connected to the story.*
If there is a photo of something in a story, the story needs to refer to that photo in some way so that the reader connects the two. An alternative to writing a long **cutline** or **copy block** under the graphic is to lose the narrative and write to the graphic. Countless studies over the years have shown that the human brain is better wired to visual images, such as photos, than to words, written or spoken. If the image does not fit the words, the brain automatically favors the image and rejects the words. The result is confusing and is a failure in storytelling.

■ *Always edit, edit.*
Clear, concise prose works. Beautiful, lengthy expositions belong in English class. It is good practice after each paragraph, after each page, after each story, to summarize each, telling the main point in one sentence.

■ *The writing toward the end of each document or page should read like the end of a movie scene.*
It should lead the reader on. If done right, the audience will *want* to click the link. This technique is used often in popular fiction: The last words in each chapter compel readers to start the next chapter, even when they can barely keep their eyes open at night.

Many writers, in trying to adjust to the rather different style required for the Web, rebel against the brevity, the compactness and the leanness of writing online. They may be reacting in part to what writer Jay David Bolter calls the "decreasing authority of the author." The transition to on-line writing is not easy for everyone. Two online sites that offer help, inspiration and tactics for writing online are Contentious (http://www.contentious.com), edited by Amy Graham, or the somewhat more grumpy site offered by Jakob Neilsen at http://www.useit.com/alertbox.

Style questions often arise for online journalists. Although the Associated Press stylebook remains the journalist's bible of style, the online world offers several other choices. One of the most notable is Wired Style, which, like the AP guide, is in paperback. Online sites include Carnegie Mellon's (http://www.cmu.edu/home/style/styleguide.html) and, for citing sources from the World Wide Web, Modern Language Association's site (http://www.mla.org/main_stl.htm). All are worthy of study as a consistent, professional look tells your audience that you are credible.

Hyperlinks

The hyperlink, or link as it is usually called, is crucial to online journalism. It deserves special attention from many angles, including writing.

Hyperlinks are doors through which a person can stroll into the Louvre (http://www.paris.org/Musees/Louvre/), then to CIA headquarters (http://www.cia.gov/cia/index.html), and end up at a friend's home page featuring the family dog. A graphic symbol—say, a picture of the Venus de Milo for the Louvre—for the link is not enough. There is a strong need for words with all links. If done well, they will capture more attention than even the glossiest advertisements.

"Here at the St. Petersburg Times," says General Manager of Web Publishing Ronald Dupont Jr., "we tried text links. And sure enough, the click-through rate was three times higher than a banner or button ad." Online journalists as well as other Web authors have all found this to be true, and repeated studies have confirmed this finding.

However, simply writing "The Louvre" with the link is ignoring the power of the Web. Journalists can use links much as broadcasters use teases for upcoming news shows. "The World's Most Famous Museum," might work. It is vital to write only teases that can deliver. Although some people would argue that the Louvre is not the world's best-known museum, many would argue that it is, and so this is a tease a journalist could use with confidence.

■ Using Video to Tell a Story

Here's a tough one for online journalism: Most journalists using the Web have come from print, print being the first medium to sense a stake being driven close to its heart. Students of journalism with little or no direct print experience will invariably be suffused with print sensibilities, whether they know it or not. The trick is to take the strong values of print to online journalism while adopting the strengths of other traditional media and of the new media growing on the Web.

Then there's that *enfant terrible* of news: TV. It stole the passion and storytelling power that newspapers had forgotten. It didn't just tell people what happened, it showed them: It was faster than an AP bulletin and right in the home. Now the Web is poised to steal all of it from TV and to combine the power of online journalism with the reliability of good newspapers, the depth of the Library of Congress and the ability to react quickly to the audience's demands.

The Web needs the biggest gun from television: the video camera. As briefly mentioned in the previous chapter, the current technological concept of video is already becoming passé. Video as we know it is going digital. There will be no more tape. Instead, images will be recorded on a hard drive and ported directly into editing machines that are greatly superior to the **analog** machines still in use at many stations. With a decent, if not professional quality, digital motion-picture camera, which can be bought for under $3,000, pictures can go directly into the computer, where they can be cropped, colored and more and then edited and stored without the loss of one **pixel** of resolution.

Bandwidth remains the biggest obstacle to full use of video. Real-time video displays 30 frames each second. The pipeline between the computer and the server hosting the Web site can't jam that much information across the street, much less across the nation. That situation will change relatively soon.

In the meantime, software developers have found some quick tricks, all based on a principal called **compression.** Compression is really subtraction. It takes frames out of the video so that instead of running through 30 in a second, it displays perhaps 15 per second. Apple's QuickTime was one of the first commercially successful compression programs. The video still takes a long time to download and the motion is jerky, but it's a start.

QuickTime VR allows more motion, including a 360-degree view of a room, for example. It's still very much a gimmick and often inappropriate for a news story. Advanced Web sites and wide bandwidth providers are using far fatter pipelines with coaxial cable and therefore can send more true video out to their customers. Fat **T-1** lines and **DSL** do about the same. And competing technologies are fast emerging. They are all headed to the same place: full bandwidth. It's a matter of who gets there first, and when.

Preparing for the full-bandwidth world is vital, and a real struggle for the legions of print-oriented journalists tinkering with the Web. It will be a defining moment for the future of news and information when high-quality video can be viewed on a computer monitor as it is now seen on television. The systems are all being put into place: digital TV, digital cameras, digital editing (also known in the industry as **nonlinear** editing).

High production values and compelling storytelling are indeed important, but the third rail that powers the news industry is quality journalism, pure and simple. Broadcast journalists need to look to the future. In online journalism, art and integrity will continue to count. You need to ready your skills to participate in that future. You do not need a $2,500 camera and a year of experience using it, but all emerging journalists should have some hands-on experience with using digital cameras and editing the pictures.

Here are some pointers to get you started:

- At news events, where you have an opportunity to actually record something happening, begin shooting your video with a wide shot. Hold it for at least 10 seconds so that the camera surveys the scene as an observer would.

- Zoom in on the heart of the action—the most important and interesting part of the event. Hold the shot, again, for at least 10 seconds. Then repeat the process from different perspectives.

These steps parallel the way people generally observe a scene. First, they visually sweep a large area quickly, seeing the context. Then they focus on the area of most interest—usually involving motion or another action. Staying on stationary shots for 10 seconds ensures having plenty of material to edit.

Professional video photographers always use a tripod (or "sticks," as they are often called) for stable shots. They also record sound whenever they are recording anything at all. A silent scene is unnatural and poor journalism.

Premiere is a software tool for downloading and editing moving pictures, which can be used to experiment with video in an online environment. It's a bit primitive, but so is the video technology on the Web right now. It promotes sensitivity to that rule of good journalism: show, don't tell. Streaming video and audio, discussed in Chapter 1, is a better way for now to use video and sound online because it allows the audience to experience the visual and audio information right away rather than having to wait for it (which many people will not do).

Even with compression technologies, download times are lengthy, and video should not be forced on the audience. The audience should be offered a choice. For example, a story about the number of airplane crashes increasing in the near future may offer the opportunity to view a plane crash. Viewers can choose to click that button and wait—a good use of the Web. But if viewers want to move on, they have that choice also.

The Power of Audio

A video of a plane crash would be odd indeed if it were silent. Unless there is a compelling reason for leaving a motion picture silent, audio should always be used with video. It's the way people take in the world.

The pure power of audio is frequently misunderstood, underrated and ignored by journalists. Even in-depth radio reporters do not make full use of audio, rightfully sensing that its power can get out of hand and that the information it provides can color a story dramatically.

The use of sound to inflame a story is a hallmark of trash or tabloid journalism and no journalist should succumb to its temptations who does not want to be a tabloid-style Web journalist. *Sound under* is an industry term for a technique all audiences have experienced. It is, for example, the ominous sound just barely within the consciousness of the audience viewing a reenactment of a bad event, such as a kidnapping. Like reenactments or dramatizations, such sounds are phony, added on, and decidedly non-journalistic. Sound under is the multimedia equivalent to doctoring quotes, manipulating photographs and extracting sound bites so they say what you want them to say, not what they were meant to say.

On the other hand, the use of genuine, natural sound, sometimes called wild sound, actually captured at the story scene is a wonderful, powerful and elegant way to communicate. Sound may accompany the photography or it may stand alone. If it's genuine and has a story to tell, let it rip.

Print-oriented students of journalism frequently misunderstand the significance of sound bites. The very term *sound bite* is often used negatively by people who think of "quotes" as important and serious. Some people believe that sound bites contain fewer words than do quotes in print (an assertion that can easily be refuted). More to the point, good reporters know that hearing the actual voice, intonation, and uncensored language of a person can do far more for a story than can a written quote lying flat on a page.

Because most of the Web audience has little access to broadband downloads and thus to high-quality sound, use of sound bites on the Web today is not compelling. On most people's computers the quality of sound is more like that of an inexpensive AM radio of 40 years ago than like the CD quality promised in the ads selling computers and software. But things will change. An increasing number of users have excellent audio systems and can employ the high fidelity available on the Net. Formats such as **MP3** promise to change much of how people use the Internet. For the most part, high-quality sound is restricted to systems using fast bandwidths, such as cable modems, so that most people, who use 28.8K modems, are left with the scratchy AM-like reproductions.

Unless the voice, the language and the quality of the recording allow and demand it, whole interviews should not be downloaded in a multimedia story. However, as with video, important parts of the sound file (the old woman explaining her story, the child squealing at a playground, the father crying at a funeral) may be made available to those who want to download it. Although the wait will certainly be shorter than it is for large video files, it will be too long to force on anyone.

The poor quality of the sound on most computers may offer some interesting opportunities. For example, a gifted NewsPort student who created and managed a well-known online journalism site experimented with using a dusty old recording of a 1923 radio announcer doing the play-by-play of one of Babe Ruth's home runs. It was a superb aspect of the story about the history of home runs.

■ Still Photography in an Age of Motion

The still photo is not dead because of the Web. There is a power in a captured moment that no motion picture can convey. Consider some of the great news images of the last half of the 20th century: the raising of the flag at Iwo Jima, the street execution of a suspected Viet Cong agent in

The Century Long Focus
Grand of 1903

Although the camera has been an integral part of journalism since the beginning of the 20th century, its ability to capture a moment so that it might be examined has not diminished. The high-end Toshiba digital camera is one of many excellent products that are moving into the future with online journalism.

Digital camera used with the permission of Toshiba.

Saigon, the Oklahoma City firefighter carrying a toddler from the bombed ruins of the federal building. Those simple, brutal and victorious moments can tell us so much more than images racing by. They are locked in our knowledge, able to be quickly referred to for generations to come.

On the other hand, journalists might do well to remember the words of Marshall McLuhan, sage of the new media: "The age of the photograph has become the age of the gesture." This Canadian communications scholar noted how the camera's images have created a world in which people see themselves not only in their everyday real actions, but also stopped in a pose (usually heroic, always dramatic) forever. This viewpoint may affect how people act—an odd thought for those who assume that journalism imitates life, not the other way around.

On the Web, and especially for journalists, the still photo has new power. The screen illuminates the photo from behind, which can add force to or wash out the image. People around the world have instant access to the image. The ability to copy the photo with a few keystrokes is invigorating to those who know that imitation is a powerful bow to talent, but it is also deeply disturbing to those worried about having their property stolen or abused.

Chapter 9 will deal more directly with copyright in the world of online journalism, but a few important issues must be acknowledged here.

Journalists must protect their integrity if their work is to have meaning. Taking images that belong to someone else without permission is a crime, legally and morally.

Because altering photos for the online world is so tantalizingly easy, journalists must adhere to tough standards when they reproduce art online. One of the primary software tools for doing this is Photoshop. Photoshop skills are easy to pick up—and hard to master. With Photoshop, you can color images, move faces from one place to another, make things that weren't there appear and make things that were there disappear.

One of the first assignments of the online journalism production course at San Francisco State University is to take a photographic or other graphic image and manipulate it with Photoshop. This task serves several purposes. It provides basic familiarity with the program, appreciation of its potential and a platform from which to discuss its dangers.

Early on, a student took the famous image of Lee Harvey Oswald being gunned down by Jack Ruby and placed a guitar, taken from a writhing Elvis Presley guitar stance, in Oswald's hands. The similarities—completely out of context—were so startling that the doctored image (not made for a news story) soon found its way across the Internet and onto many bulletin boards across the Web. This situation provided an opportunity to discuss an important point: Altering any information, visual or otherwise, to make it significantly different from the reality is a crime against real journalism. Period. However, cropping a photo, fixing the color to depict the scene more accurately, and taking out imperfections in the reproduction that have nothing to do with the story are acceptable.

■ Graphics Getting Graphic

One rule guides the use of graphics on the Web and elsewhere: Graphics must be instantly understandable. No exceptions. The temptation to use complex graphics is great in online journalism, predominantly because they are so easy to find and drop in. Once again, however, journalists must remember that they are storytellers and that they will fail in this role if their story is not understood. Because of the great ease and even temptation to click off a story and go somewhere else on the Net, journalists have even greater motivation to keep their stories clean, visibly simple, attractive and important.

The most evident graphic on the Web is letters, or, as they are known in the online world, fonts.

Just about everyone who begins making Web pages has had the fun of playing with fonts. First you try the 𝔒𝔩𝔡 𝔈𝔫𝔤𝔩𝔦𝔰𝔥 style because it's so newspapery. Then you use something like *Sanvito* for your byline because your name looks so darn good that way. After a while, the page is a mess with styles and people leave, usually without knowing exactly why.

The next chapter deals with fonts and other important design issues in depth but it's good to start thinking about some basic rules for online graphics, starting with fonts: First, make sure the font can be read easily, without any confusion. Among other things that means no italics. It is extremely difficult to read italic fonts on the screen. This important rule is too often unconsidered or ignored.

The best fonts for online use may be sans serif, which means they don't have the little curlicues on the ends. This R is set in a font with feet on the left ends. This R has no feet; it is sans serif. Sans serif fonts tend to be easier to read online according to many Web designers.

Bulleted, or "unordered," lists are one more primary tool for online journalism and are often the best way to present information in an online journalism site. They usually look something like this:

The budget calls for:

- $150 billion for health and welfare
- $100 billion for defense
- $50 billion for transportation

Numbered, or "ordered," lists also work well online. They convey complex information at a glance and have the added benefit of identifying a clear priority.

For example, in a story about the governor's vetoing budget items that cost too much and do too little (in the governor's opinion), a numbered list can convey the governor's priorities.

1. $20 million cut in the mosquito abatement allocation. The governor said he eradicated parasites in his first term.
2. $15 million cut in the marsh restoration budget. The governor said he paved over the marshes at the beginning of his second term and it killed all the mosquitoes.
3. $5 million added to the Mosquito Abatement Workers Widows and Orphans fund. The governor said he regrets the enormous number of suicides among former mosquito abatement employees.

The format is simple, clean and great for online glancers. Links from these lists can take people to more depth and context.

The most basic and therefore most important graphic formats used in an introduction to online journalism, aside from words, are called GIFs and JPEGs. GIF (pronounced by the old school as "jiff"; more recently pronounced with a hard *g*, as in "glad") stands for graphics interchange format and was the first format used to display graphics online. GIFs remain, for the time being, the standard and the best choice for images, such as logos, that do not require great precision. (There is reason to believe that GIFs will be replaced, because of legal squabbles, with a format called *PNG*, pronounced "ping.")

JPEG (pronounced "jay-peg") stands for Joint Photographic Experts Group and was developed a little later to make up for the lack of very clear images needed for such graphics as photographs. JPEGs are also smaller than GIFs, taking up less file size in the story, which is an important aspect of production.

The greater the size of a file on a Web page, the longer it will take for an audience to download it. Many people, especially those just starting out on the Web, are under the impression that the greater the file size, the better the image, but that's becoming less true every year. The next chapter will discuss the issue of file size in greater depth.

One last word about GIFs: some are animated, that is, they move. This is especially important to online journalism if only because it is one of the key factors that separate online journalism from the static printed world of newspapers and magazines (and books, for that matter). Motion for motion's sake is rarely advisable, but when it helps tells the story and tells it better than would adding another 250 words of copy, it's key.

Animated GIFs are rapidly losing their popularity among high-end Web authors because of newer and better technologies, such as Flash, developed by Macromedia, authors of Director, and its subset, Shockwave.

Journalists would do best to consider these graphics tools in the second stage of Web production rather than in an introductory phase. Where to put graphics and how big (or small) they should be are issues for Chapter 6. Journalists are concerned with accurate, fair and complete images that provide real information. A JPEG of a redwood tree will tell the viewer more and tell it far faster than a paragraph that describes the tree's appearance. Making the JPEG of the tree a link, which allows the audience to see a forest, or the root structure of a redwood forest or how the roots lashed together just under the forest floor provide great strength makes for genuine online journalism. But if the image is not clear, easy to spot and easy to understand, the journey with the audience is over before it starts.

Tables, for the builder of Web pages, are an especially important tool. Although a little more work to learn—and a great deal more work to master—they are an important tool for the beginning online journalist to learn because they are perhaps the single best way to layout a page. Tables provide flexibility and power to any layout and must not be ignored. Tables also allow you to build charts, exploit data from spreadsheets and otherwise clearly present parts of a story. Like all the basics of online journalism, the coding for tables is readily attainable.

Image maps help journalists tell a complicated story quickly and well. Although they are called maps, image maps are not necessarily maps of a place. Image maps are a way for journalists to put anything they want, usually links, on a page, to enable people to visualize the story more clearly.

For example, a story about a particularly dangerous community in which several killings and other acts of violence have occurred might include an aerial photograph of the neighborhood with links in each spot where a crime took place. Each link could take the audience to the individual story. In a story about airplane safety, an illustration of the aircraft's cockpit control panel could be made into an image map. By clicking on different parts of the panel,x the audience could find out what all those meters and knobs and handles do. Image maps provide context and particulars visually.

Interactivity in Journalism

Let's take the story about airplane safety a step further. Through the image map of the cockpit controls a person will be able to fly that plane. If the person pulls back on the wheel the view out the window alters to suggest that the plane is going up. Then the fuel gauge indicator suddenly shows that the tank is empty. The person must now turn on the reserve tank or the view from the window is going to show that the plane is speeding to earth. The mysterious and overused word *interactivity* is now very much a part of the story.

People have always interacted with the media. Magazine readers complete a quiz and then turn to another page for the answers. Television viewers become disgusted with the local newscast and turn the TV off with a yell. Crossword-puzzle addicts interact with the newspaper daily.

Interactivity can be far more flexible and deep in online journalism. For example, after seeing a story on NewsPort about how deeply Microsoft had penetrated the software market, two very able students created a program asking readers to fill in all the software tools they used at school, home and work. After filling in the information, people could press a button to find out how much money they had given to Bill Gates (http://NewsPort.sfsu.edu/archive/s97/ms/index.html). The story immediately had personal implications for the readers on top of the larger economic and social matters it discussed in depth.

Throughout, this book has dealt with the interactive nature of online journalism. Interactivity can be as elementary as a chatroom on a news site where the audience can go to respond to the story, whether it's about O. J. Simpson or the local weather. It can be as complex as your imagination and skills will allow. It may be an invitation for members of the audience to post their own multimedia responses, in music, painting and poetry, to a debate about a topic such as war in the Balkans. Perhaps it's an e-mail service allowing people to automatically receive news items of special interest to them, such as sports scores or stock exchange numbers. Quizzes and games are a way to attract and retain an audience, allowing online journalists to disseminate the news and information they have collected. Some online news sites have considered inviting readers to write their own obituaries in advance (although staff would have to check the facts and verify the accounts to make these pieces worthy of a genuine journalism publication).

Whatever else they offer, all online news sites that have the time, equipment and expertise to do so should offer a search function. Consider the last three times you went to an online news site on your own. Did you go there to see what sort of news you could find or were you seeking something specific? Chances are, it was the latter. Most people go to online news sites with a specific mission in mind, not for a leisurely reading of the day's news. The fast and efficient way for people to find what they want is by using a search function. News sites that do not have this interactive element will lose their audience to those that do. Not only should this search function be a priority, but should play prominently on the front page.

Creating search functions has long been restricted to those with access to complicated software programs such as CGI scripting. Webmasters need to have basic understanding of the server they are working with, whether it's a Windows NT box or Macintosh. They may also need to know an advanced computing language, such as PERL, Visual Basic or AppleScript. A search function is a valuable tool, and one that doesn't come easily.

The temptation to create an interactive component to a story often prompts online journalists to think first of a rather complicated procedure using software tools that are inaccessible to them. Yet, there are good tools right beneath their noses. A wonderful case in point was an online story about diving for a navy ship that sank during World War II. The producers of the story used the scroll bar on every Web browser to allow readers to dive down to the shipwreck. On the way, they passed other landmarks indicating just how deep they had gone: Mount Everest turned upside down would be here, the Titanic would be here, all light would cease here. Readers scrolled down and down until they reached the navy ship. The tool provided real news, perspective and true interactivity.

It's not always easy to get interactivity to work in a story the way you want. And interactivity for its own sake can be overdone. The audience needs a clear way to get through the story—a sort of narrative. In a medium that measures use in seconds, people are likely to leave if faced with too many choices. The next chapter will introduce some ways to build interactivity into a story.

Where Are the New Storytellers?

JANE ELLEN STEVENS

In 1997, I worked for New York Times Television on a TV program called "Science Times," which appeared on The Learning Channel. The program was loosely based on the newspaper's science section. We reporters were a new breed of journalists: mostly newspaper science writers, equipped with digital video cameras, who went on scientific expeditions. Each of us became video person, field producer, sound person, reporter, writer—and, sometimes, talent—all wrapped into one.

My epiphany in multimedia journalism occurred on one of these expeditions. It was a month-long oceanographic voyage on the research ship *Atlantis,* whose scientists were exploring all known deep-sea volcanic vents along the Mid-Atlantic Ridge. I dove more than a mile to the bottom of the ocean on the deep-sea submersible Alvin. My main job was to return with video for a "Science Times" segment. But I also wrote a traditional news story for the newspaper section and provided text, still photographs, graphics information and video clips for Cyber-Times, the part of the New York Times Web site that produces its own content instead of relying on the newspaper's reporters.

While the scientists on board the Atlantis were discovering new species and new vent fields, I discovered two things that would change my life: (1) My digital camera had become my reporter's notebook, from which I could draw stills, video, text and information for graphics, and (2) one person could provide most of the elements necessary to tell a story in multimedia.

As the story appeared on the CyberTimes site (www.nytimes.com/library/cyber/week/dive-index.html), it was disjointed—video clips in one place, a photo gallery in another, text running alongside a few photos and graphics in another.

Rob Fixmer, then editor of CyberTimes, and I decided to try to take it one step further. We worked with a computer whiz to figure out what information in a story works best delivered in text, what works best in video and audio, what works best in graphics and weave these elements together in an integrated, seamless, graceful format. But after we designed it we were told that if it were put on the Times' Web site, the whole system would crash. The effort fizzled when I left NYT-TV to move into multimedia reporting, Fixmer returned to the business section of the Times to become technology editor, and the computer whiz abandoned newspapers for law school.

But that wasn't why the Times never pursued this type of storytelling further. Convincing the Times to adopt modern technology is like pushing a snake. What the under-30 Web geeks in another building do when they put the newspaper's stories on the Times' Web site is of little concern to the reporters at the Times. That's not to say that the Times isn't interested in multimedia; I think that like most newspapers, it's just not moving fast enough.

And here's the meat of this nut: Every newspaper should be training one or two reporters in every section or beat—sports, health, politics, education, crime, and so on—to use a digital video camera and require that they use it on every story they report. They should be taught to think visually for every story they produce and to abandon words when graphics or video or stills work better. Editors should be working with the reporters to produce stories for the Web site directly from the newsroom, not sending text to people who simply add graphics or photos and have no training in journalism and no knowledge of the stories that are coming to them.

And every television organization should be hiring full-time beat reporters who produce the content (video, stills, text and information for graphics) and design stories from beginning to end.

It's not an easy undertaking, but it's necessary if newspapers want to survive and if journalism is to continue in its role as one of the cornerstones of democracy, that is, giving people enough information to make informed decisions about their lives. The task is made more daunting because of the need to figure out how to morph the two major approaches to putting a story together into multimedia.

The first approach makes up the heart and soul of journalistic tradition. In this approach, the story resides in the head of the journalist. The editor helps the story along but doesn't dictate its content. Experienced reporters who specialize in feature and investigative stories on politics, business, science, technology, the arts and local communities know their beats better than anyone and can tell their stories better than anyone.

Take this approach into multimedia, where journalists carry a digital video camera and send back text, stills and video, and you could call it the Max Headroom method of multimedia storytelling. ("Max Headroom," if you don't remember, was a TV series in which a journalist roamed the streets and ferreted out stories that he sent back to his network via his video camera. He was aided most of the time by his alter ego in the computer system.)

There's another approach to reporting. This type of reporting is most characteristic of television news. The story resides in the head of the producer, who assigns a researcher, a writer (who is sometimes also the reporter), a camera crew, and an editor to it. These people provide the pieces that the producer puts together into a coherent whole. For breaking stories—earthquakes, floods, school shootings, fast wars, car chases, as well as sports—there's no better model. Newspapers adapt this model to report local disaster or crisis stories.

Take this approach into multimedia and you could call it the "Snow Crash" method. In Neal Stephenson's book of the same name, the main character, Hiro Protagonist, was, among other things, a stringer for the Central Intelligence Corporation (CIC). He sent bits of information, music, movies and microcodes to CIC, but he never knew how it was going to fit into the whole story.

Broadcast TV Web sites (CNN, MSNBC.com, ABCNEWS.com) and one newspaper Web site (USA Today) use the Snow Crash method. Pieces of video, text, stills and graphics are put together by a producer. It's a great method that takes advantage of the Web's fast-fast-fast up-to-the-minute characteristic.

An example of a good use of the Snow Crash method is the coverage provided by CNN, ABCNEWS.com and MSNBC.com of the spate of hurricanes that hit the East Coast in 1999. They combined breaking-news text, maps, hurricane history, videos of flying through the eye of a hurricane, real-time tracking information, advice on what to do in hurricanes and an alert service, if requested, into an informative and useful package assembled from dozens of sources by a producer. The coverage by The New York Times paled by comparison—one reporter wrote a story that appeared as text on the Web site. Not even a single map was used.

As the pipe gets bigger, as broadband provides the ability to weave the characteristics of this new medium into seamless, interactive storytelling, the Snow Crash method isn't going to be enough for the in-depth investigative or continual coverage of a beat. Because the Web is also about greater depth than was previously possible, and presented in ways that have also never been possible.

An example of a "Max Headroom" approach is being developed by Discovery Channel's Web site in a year-long initiative during 2000 to report on hate and violence in the United States. This approach could be adapted by every U.S. newspaper and local television station for its local crime beat. It could be adapted by the national news organizations for a national crime beat. Discovery is developing a shell—the context in which to put all stories—on the subject of violence. Included in the shell are standing components: national data on different types of crime (graphics); a place for people to assess their level of risk for being victims of a particular type of crime (interactive); crime-prevention resources (text and graphics); public service announcements put together by youth (video) with links to the kids who made the videos; and chat rooms for people who want to exchange information on violence prevention.

Stories—about communities that have decreased crime, about research into what makes healthy communities, about the people who have helped make those changes, about projects that have worked and those that haven't—will be told with a mix of text, stills, video and graphics. Breaking stories—school shootings, office shootings and the like—will be put into the shell, with integrated links to information that puts the events into context, spells out the economic and emotional consequences to families and communities, provides information on the latest research, and examines prevention programs. One reporter, an expert in violence epidemiology, is developing the content and design for this Web site. She is working with graphics editors and a producer in the same way that a beat reporter works with graphics people, photographers and an editor in a newspaper.

If this site were put together by a producer who knew little about the subject, it would come out looking more like a poor television program—a good review with insufficient depth for people to take action on the information provided.

News organizations must make an investment in reporters who can provide depth, who hold the story in their heads, who provide that personal link to a story, who deliver it in text, video and audio and inter-active graphics, and who can interact with readers. They must begin to identify which stories reside in the heads of editors or producers, which are controlled by reporters and when in the life of a developing story it's appropriate to run each type. They've got to start training reporters and editors to think about breaking down their stories into text, graph-ics, video, stills, audio and interactive elements.

The Washington Post recently told its reporters to begin thinking about the fact that they were going to have to pick up a video camera and begin doing their stories in a different way. The groans could be heard from coast to coast.

It's not too early—in fact, we're approaching the time when it's a bit late—to make that investment, to understand the necessary skills, how long it takes to train reporters, how their work integrates with that of graphics editors, copy editors, and Web design editors. All it takes is a few multimedia-savvy reporters to show that it may be a challenge, but it's not impossible.

And this approach provides a new way of reporting information that the public can use, really use, rather than information that merely entertains or leaves people hanging.

Jane Ellen Stevens is a freelance multimedia journalist. She began her career at the Boston Globe, moved to the San Francisco Examiner, and founded a syndicated science and technology feature service with clients that included the Los Angeles Times, the Dallas Morn-ing News, the Washington Post, and Asahi Shimbun's AERA Magazine. For four years, she lived and worked in Kenya and Indonesia. She has written for magazines, including National Geographic, and worked for New York Times Television as a videojournalist.

chapter 6

Convergence

*I do not mean to be the slightest bit critical of TV newspeople,
who do a superb job, considering that they operate under severe
time constraints and have the intellectual depth of hamsters. But
TV news can only present the "barebones" of a story; it takes a
newspaper, with its capability to present vast amounts of
information, to render the story truly boring.*
—Dave Barry

On the World Wide Web you are the top dog and the bottom dog.
You are also the middle dog. In short, all the jobs that once you
coveted, scorned and performed are all yours at some stage.

You are the general manager of the broadcast station, the
publisher of the newspaper. But you are also the reporter, the editor and the producer. Sometimes you are the janitor. As the Web
develops, an appreciation of all these roles will come more and
more into focus. In a sense, the much-discussed convergence of
media is also manifesting itself in the convergence of the many
roles you may find yourself assuming. What tools do you have at
your disposal to carry out this new work? What tools are in production and may be available in the near future? These questions
are explored straight ahead.

■ Design Online

Now journalists have the power at their fingertips to make both mistakes referred to by Dave Barry in the epigraph. Or we can start fresh and make neither. Which will it be?

This book has referred to multimedia as a new medium combining all traditional mass media: words, graphics, video, audio and now a deep, serious and immediate level of interactivity. The journalist's task is to take the strengths of each component and leave the weaknesses behind. This powerful new creation will bring dangers, opportunities and consequences as yet unimagined.

For the past generations of reporters and editors, who railed against publishers, it's time to give it up. Now all journalists are publishers. At this early stage of the World Wide Web journalists are often forced to decide not only whom to interview, which documents to mention in the story and what photograph to include, but also where on the page a photograph will be placed, what font will be used for the text and even whether advertisements will appear on the page. This power brings a commensurate responsibility. Journalists must be thoughtful but speedy, cautious but adventurous, comprehensive but discriminate. In short, breathtaking challenges lie ahead for online journalists.

Journalists are in the information business. The information they specialize in is arguably among the most important—news. And the audience that comes for news is very much subject to the broader information journalists convey, consciously or not.

For example, when people pick up a New York Times, they know they are picking up news from a serious organization. The Times' publishers and editors want this message conveyed, and readers understand it instantly from the paper's classic clean and spare lines.

When TV viewers tune in a show such as "Hard Copy," they expect information that will electrify, entertain and (perhaps) edify them, because the producers have given them this message graphically.

When people go online, they also get visual information about what to expect. Since you are now reporter, editor, producer *and* publisher when you build your online news stories and sites, you must consider the visual information you are sending to your audience. The challenges are sometimes daunting, often exciting, but always vitally important.

Here are 10 basic points to keep in mind when laying out a page on the World Wide Web:

10-Point Checklist for Web Design

■ *Is there one central eye-catching element on each page (roughly twice as big as any other screen element)?*
Perhaps the banner across the top is that element. Maybe your lead story or the graphic accompanying the lead feature piece instead of the hard news piece prominently played.

■ *Is there an overwhelming element on the page that is* not *the main point of the page?*
The eye will naturally scout the page looking for a place to land. Research conducted for the Poynter Institute (http://www.poynter.org) suggests that Web users scan pages from left to right. And they do so in seconds, usually resting on the element that is strongest—biggest, most colorful, or most arresting emotionally, for instance. You must decide whether that's where you want the audience to focus first and foremost, and you must be able to say why. ("Because it's a cool GIF and I spent all night working on it," is not an appropriate answer.)

■ *Is there a* clear *visual hierarchy, or do people's eyes roam around wildly looking for a place to focus?*
Newspaper icon Joseph Pulitzer was among the first in the news business to fully understand and exploit a visual hierarchy. He understood, even before sophisticated research bore out his conclusions, that newspaper readers' eyes scan from upper left to lower right, then to lower left, then to upper right. Pulitzer's headlines were massive; his layout brought the reader's eyes quickly to the upper right of the front page, where he played the big (i.e., biggest selling point) story of the day. Readers must quickly see what you consider the most interesting and important stories. This information will tell them much about you and whether they want to stay in your company.

■ *Do the size and weight of the graphic elements vary?*
A page full of graphic elements, such as photos, all of the same size or weight, will cause the audience to look for the visual hierarchy. If it's not there, the audience will assume everything is of equal importance and won't know where to start. Faced with this difficulty, they may simply click to another site.

■ *Are the colors complementary?*
Purples and greens look awful together and may not deliver the information about your story you want to deliver. Get a color wheel and

keep it visible. More sophisticated backgrounds using color are often achieved through a process called tiling (you choose the color and it repeats across the area you define, like tiles on a floor).

■ *Are the colors and tones in keeping with the mood and point of the story?* The colors may be somber if your story is somber, but grays against blacks may strain the reader's eyes and prompt a getaway click. Choose tones and colors that suit the story (and site)—but that also will help keep the audience with you.

■ *Does each page have a texture or depth?* This is a tough one, especially for people just starting out (although the display of stories has texture in any medium). Only in rare instances would an absolutely flat page be appropriate—saying, perhaps, this is a really silly, fun piece; there's nothing to it. But by simply using contrasting colors you can make some elements pop out and others hang back. Put yellow (though gold is better because it has more depth, or texture) on a blue field and the yellow will appear to be over the blue background, giving some dimension, or depth.

■ *Does the text completely avoid the use of italics?* Again, italics do not work online. Period. The resolutions are even worse than for nonitalic text; the words slant into the following words (requiring more pixels of space, hardly worth the coding trouble) and italics are unnecessary. Underline, capitalize, use boldface—anything—but don't use italics.

■ *Is the text limited to 10–15 words across the screen?* Try reading across a computer screen from one side to the other, especially when the font is small nine-point characters. When you get to the end of the line, you are likely to have trouble moving down to the correct next line because your eye gets lost. Many thoughtful designers do not allow any more than 10 words per line. If the fonts are at least 14 points in size that rule can be stretched a bit. Many of the browsers people use at home automatically drop the size to nine-point type unless the fonts are part of a graphic, which, unfortunately, increases the size of the page and the download speeds. The intelligent compromise is to write tight, lean and bright (see Chapter 5).

■ *Are the links strong, clear teases with words?* Avoid using a graphic without words as a link. Even if there's a blue border around the graphic, people will have to think about whether it's a link and whether they want to go to it. In the seconds it takes to make this decision, readers will be lost. Again, research has shown that links that include words are far more effective than are links that use only graphics. Always try to avoid the "click here" line at a link. It's a poor excuse for not being able to write a sharp invitation to go on. The cliff-hanger tactic described in the last chapter works: Write teases as a prompt for the audience to go on to the next part of the story. Broadcast news also has something to teach here—at the end of a segment, just before the commercial break, viewers are invited to stay to see other interesting and important stories. The break in the action at the end of a book chapter, the conclusion of a movie scene and the end of a TV show segment are equivalent to the end of a Web page requiring a click. Make it work for you.

■ Fitting the Multiples Into a Medium

Like artisans who use tools to assemble a work of utility, power and beauty, journalists use their tools to turn writing, graphics and sound into a carefully crafted story. In assembling any artful news story, whether it's a 15-column-inch print obituary or a minute-thirty broadcast package, the trick to doing it well is to give some disciplined thought to the process before beginning. Some of the key questions journalists must consider are:

- What is this story really about?
- What *must* be in it?
- What are the least important and interesting elements?
- What is the appropriate tone of the story?
- What will the audience remember?

The next step is to look at the storytelling, or production, elements that can be used to tell the story. The major questions about how the site and the stories should look and feel remain to be answered. Is the broadcast metaphor the best way to do that? How can we make it easy, interesting and attractive to use? Do we want to look like a newspaper online?

Take a look at nonnewspaper sites that are easy, clean and attractive to use. A good example of such a site is a big commercial site like Sony (http://www.sony.com). Ask yourself why your site has to look like every other hard-to-use news site rather than like an easy-to-use commercial site. Look at a state-of-the-art designer's site, such as Vivid (http://www. vivid.com), to see what professional Web designers do in their own work.

It may be tempting to try to stuff 10 pounds of news into a five-pound bag. But if highly successful nonnews sites can resist that urge, news sites can too. The hyperlink is the key to avoiding jamming too much into one Web page.

The disciplined use of the abundant space in a site is key. Journalists need to remember that using the Web is different from reading a paper, magazine or book. It's more like "reading" a poster, a comic book or a photograph. Restrictions of those media require the audience to grasp the message in different ways. A poster is a particularly good example of conveying visual information quickly. The best ones convey complex information in an arresting fashion with few words. You can borrow ideas from these media as you design Web pages.

Although an online news site will inevitably use words, when you design a site you should think about the writing *last*. Think about how you would tell the story if you were not allowed to write. What images and sounds are available? An exercise that can be immensely valuable is considering how a radio journalist, using nothing but natural sound (no words read by the reporter), would tell the story? What about a movie maker? What would a billboard show? Rather than thinking of the writing as the bricks, make it the mortar that keeps the other elements together. Always remember that reading on the Web for sustained periods is difficult.

A useful tool borrowed from the film industry is the storyboard. Strictly speaking, a storyboard is a well-thought-out and well-drawn set of scenes, exactly what the audience will see on the screen. Your drawing abilities do not have to rival Picasso's; you need merely sketch out, as best you can, what you aim to show.

The essential accompaniment to this exercise is the site map, or what some people refer to as the information architecture. How many separate Web pages (also known as documents) will you build? How will they link together? Will there be a navigation bar? This map will change, naturally, as your reporting brings back new, better information. You may scrap your entire concept and start from scratch if the story warrants it.

For the genuine journalist there is one thing and only one thing important in the work: the story. Ninety-nine percent of the time the solution to problems, quandaries and dilemmas can be easily seen if you simply ask yourself, *What is best for the story?* Not what's best for you, your teacher, your editor, your executive producer or publisher, but what's best for the story.

The storyboard is a tool that comes to us from the movie industry. On a storyboard each scene is displayed graphically, traditionally with a drawing or sketch, so filmmakers can plan exactly what they want to see and when they want to see it. In the online world, the storyboard is electronic. Many excellent software tools are available, such as StoryBoard Quick.

Courtesy PowerProduction Software Inc., www.powerproduction.com.

What Works Right Now

So many wonderful software and hardware tools are available now that it is more important than ever to remember that the more that is loaded onto a page, the longer it will take for the page to download. Waiting to download is what people are upset about when they whine about the "World Wide Wait."

The most important factor is file size. In general, *no Web page should be larger than 50K total; 25K is far better.*

You may complain that everyone should be on a T-1 line or using cable modem, but the reality (and as a student of journalism, reality does not frighten you) is that most Web users are still using their basic telephone lines and modems that connect at 28.8 or even 14.4 bits per second.

The chart here is posted throughout the NewsPort lab to remind everyone of this reality. The times account for real-world delays in **routers, switches** and busy **networks.**

Connection	25K	50K	100K	500K
14.4 bps	30 seconds	1 minute	2 minutes	6 minutes
28.8 bps	20 seconds	40 seconds	1.5 minutes	3 minutes
33.6 bps	15 seconds	30 seconds	1 minute	2.5 minutes
56 bps	10 seconds	20 seconds	40 seconds	2 minutes
ISDN, T-1, DSL and Cable Modem	Less than 1 second	Less than 1 second	2 seconds	6 seconds

As just illustrated, another excellent way to deliver news and information today is with a table. Tables are easy to build and quick to download. Other available options, described previously, are bulleted lists and GIFs and JPEGs file formats. Photoshop is a terrific software program that allows users to make images better—and slimmer. Sound files can be relatively slim and very effective. Audio can, however, have unintended or inappropriate editorial power (see Chapter 4). Audio is also a fiercely protected medium in copyright law, a subject explored in Chapter 9.

Java continues its slow creep up the Web food chain. There are two basic kinds: pure Java and JavaScript. The full-powered Java involves a rather complicated programming language. Unless you are very comfortable with lots of coding and have tried your hand successfully at real programming, it's best to start with JavaScript.

JavaScript allows you to create tools such as a scrolling ticker, resembling the displays under bank signs or in subway stations that tell the news. It is also behind popular tools such as **mouseovers** or what some Web authors refer to as interactive images. It is a strong alternative to complicated interactive scripting such as CGI, another set of tasks outside the scope of most Web authors. It takes drive and aptitude to attach JavaScript, but the rewards are significant.

One day the full-bore Java language may do what it has promised: make it unnecessary to write different code for different browsers and different kinds of computers. Certainly the people who developed the language in 1991 at Sun Microsystems would like to believe that it will (and have others believe it so their stock prices will rise). Whether this will happen remains to be seen. There is plenty of competition already and many new twists and turns ahead.

■ Preparing for What Will Work Tomorrow

The most exciting part of online journalism is the future. The technical bogeyman is bandwidth. The previous chart tells the story. In five to 10 years, the chart will fade away and journalists will be able to use audio, video and even 3-D images in coding such as **VRML** (Virtual Reality Markup Language, pronounced VER-mel) with far fewer worries. But these opportunities will also bring problems, so preparation is key.

Imagine for a few minutes what it will be like when well-equipped and skilled journalists will be able to tell a story with all the power and promise of a fully realized World Wide Web.

A jumbo jet leaves New York City headed for Europe and disappears over the ocean, inexplicably. The authorities are notified, an alert newsperson hears the call on a police scanner. A quick confirmation with the FAA and the airline company sets the story in play.

The speed of the Internet allows the newsteam to send e-mail news to subscribers (some of whom may be getting ready to board a plane at JFK). The actual audio from the scanner is recorded and made available. Maps using satellite imaging are immediately constructed. A database of previous accidents is loaded. Photos of a jet of the same type are dropped in, perhaps with schematics of the construction. Video comes in from the airport, where people are learning of the accident, all live. Cameras are also recording events at the destination. Previous disappearances in the same area are linked. The opportunities are as great as your imagination, budget and stamina.

What is being created is an unparalleled medium of immediacy and depth and choice. Journalists can choose to be part of it or not. Many tools being forged right now may or may not be widely adopted by Web developers. **Cascading style sheets,** save time by allowing a change on one document to be repeated on relevant pages. With **DHTML,** or dynamic HTML, Web authors may be able to program changes in a story that would take effect automatically. This is especially important for newspeople working in a breaking news situation, where events can rapidly turn. If your online news site is already set to adapt to changes—such as a live person suddenly turning up dead, a volcano suddenly going from a smoky stage to an explosive one or a person on trial suddenly being acquitted—having computer codes that will allow you to plug in those changes without having to totally rewrite your HTML might be wonderful.

XML, short for *eXtensible Markup Language,* could make HTML obsolete because it is easy to use and can be used everywhere, including on **WebTV.** Better yet for online journalists, XML promises the ability to use search engines in a way that will make information retrieval faster, more efficient and more accurate than it is now. As if these possibilities weren't enough, several major news organizations have proposed a new coding standard called *News Industry Text Format,* or **NITF.** NITF would work in the XML code but would have the added advantage of setting a single standard for all news pages, which could make it possible to move news stories around the Internet. For the online journalists of the 21st century, this development could certainly be a benefit. Yet there are already legitimate complaints that news Web pages are too much like factory-produced templates, and NITF may further this trend. The large media groups behind the plan, naturally, like the notion because it appears to be a short-term money saver. Whether it would cause problems in the long term remains to be seen.

Finally, there is WebTV itself, which seems to be floundering a bit after a much hyped start. Will people want to use the Web on a television set? Probably. Will they want to use it the way it looks now, with lots of words and no real-time video? Probably not.

If convergence remains a buzzword among people concerned and interested in the future of the news media, there is ample reason. It is said that Americans own more televisions per household than they have toilets. TV monitors are no longer restricted to living rooms, but are commonly found in bedrooms, kitchens and recreation rooms as well. They may be the precursors to screens for the Internet in all these locations. The ability to network, or link, these monitors is relatively available and affordable. And good voice-recognition systems will soon be available to take the place of the television remote control and the computer mouse.

In the future, rather than simply turning on the TV and sitting down for a one-way (the TV's way) show, a growing audience will use voice commands to tell the monitor to display a TV news show, a movie or entertainment program and will skip from one program to another at will. Voice

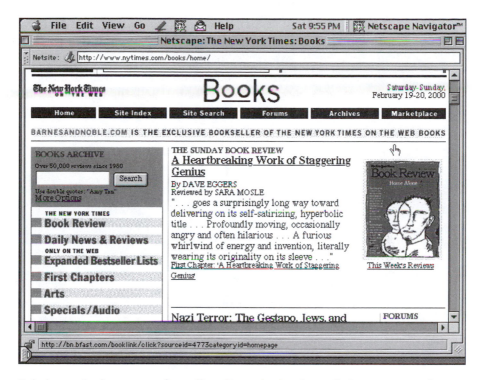

It is increasingly common for online sites, whether journalistic or not, to allow the audience to make purchases right on the site. The New York Times, for example, has a place set aside on its online book review pages for people to purchase titles from Barnes & Noble. Typically the hosting site (in this case, the New York Times) gets a share of the purchase price.

commands will enable people to stop and dig more deeply through subjects as they please, accessing the Internet through these same monitors. Print-outs and musical programming will also be available, as will the commercial transactions that currently push profits on Web sites selling everything from stocks to groceries.

For traditional broadcast news this fragmentation will make the current declining share of network viewing in the face of cable look downright silly. For newspapers, the concerns may be greater. The paper itself, as an attractive, portable and thoroughly viable medium will probably not disappear. But the consistent loss of audience through most of the 20th century has no reason to abate.

What will, what *can,* newspapers do? Peoria, Illinois, journalist Tom Mangan put it well: "What does the newspaper industry have up its sleeve when convergence happens? Are we really done for because we have limited experience in delivering content via sound and video?" Mangan posted this inquiry on a popular Listserv for journalists, one that hundreds of reporters, editors, producers and publishers read each day. No one posted a reply.

Converging Cyberjournalism

FRED STEFANY

Convergence, the blending of different media, is one of the most used and least understood terms in almost every article on the future of news and information. Most people say that video is blending with print; that the result can be found on the Internet now and will be found on interactive TV in the future. Although technology will allow this to happen, it's not clear what people actually want. In today's competitive world the leaders in delivering convergent media cannot afford to wait to find out what people want. So what skills should journalists develop and how should they work with their various media? They should give as many choices as possible in a credible manner, monitor the audience's behavior and adjust quickly. The Internet allows journalists to combine the benefits of print and video to offer many choices. It is also a great tracking mechanism for seeing what people actually view and it provides instant feedback. Still, many companies are having a difficult time implementing these recommendations.

Convergence has ramifications for many aspects of journalism. Millions of people will publish "news and information" with their digital cameras and personal opinions. The best stuff usually wins. Good journalists will always find an audience. The downside is that the number of people who think a particular journalist is good will decrease as people find their niche sources. The Internet allows people to put together their favorite sources, which fragments the journalistic society. Readers who used to get all their news from the New York Times can now just as easily get headlines from the Times, sports from USA Today, and weather from the Weather Channel.

Another effect of convergence relates to the journalistic responsibility of blending "need to know" stories with "want to know" stories. This trade-off will still exist, but in a different form. Journalists must develop stories for both approaches and give the choice to their audience. Some people want news tailored for them and others want to be told what is important. Recognizing this situation will allow journalists to adapt their style to the changing landscape.

The type of journalism practiced needs to be viewed in a new light. Traditionally, people studied print or broadcast journalism and developed the corresponding attitude: print considering depth more important and broadcast considering timeliness more important. But people will view what they want in the manner in which they want to view it.

So, do journalists have to cover everything the viewers want? Almost, but not quite. Human behavior changes slowly, and people do agree on many trends. Journalists can make their lives easier, by adapting their own style to these trends.

One of the trends people agree on is that their lives are getting busier. Journalists who offer the audience a quick story with the ability to drill down for more depth, interact and have fun will have a larger audience because they are allowing people to absorb the information in their own way.

Some people want the lean-back feeling of an evening newscast, whereas others prefer the organization of a newspaper. Both media will continue on longer than many people are predicting. However, they will lose a lot of mind-share to services that combine the best of both and also add interactivity.

Interactivity is an important journalistic device. It gets people to come back for more and in some cases it can add to the original story, keeping the audience involved and building loyalty to the journalist and the service. Also, by making news and information a little more entertaining, interactivity leads the audience to make more of the day available for news.

Giving people what they want and allowing them to digest news and information in the way they want seems intuitively the right way to proceed. But what does that say about journalism? Will all stories take on the look and feel of the lowest common denominator? Will the American public become less knowledgeable about the real issues going on in the world? How will people know what to believe with the millions of choices that are on the horizon?

There are, indeed, risks in giving more choices to the audience. But choices must be given. It is very important to establish your credibility as a journalist or news service. Give choices of stories, formats and styles, but maintain your angle and image. Those who enjoy what they see will promote it and you will gain a following. A smaller, adamant following in a bigger potential audience will be a success in tomorrow's sea of choices.

Fred Stefany is chief operating officer and chief financial officer for ReacTV, the first provider of personalized video newscasts. ReacTV adds layers of depth and interactivity to video news before repurposing it as a customized video newscast for viewers via the Internet. He received his M.B.A. from the Sloan School of the Massachusetts Institute of Technology and a B.S. in engineering from Lehigh University.

chapter 7

Multimedia Editing

Near the end of the reporting and production process comes a step that distinguishes all real journalists—they go back over their work with fresh eyes and ears in the all important edit.

There is much more to this than just making sure the typos are gone, the spelling is correct and the links work. They must make sure that they have accomplished the goals they set out to reach. Even more important, they must be certain that vital intangibles, such as keeping on a straight and narrow ethical track, are held true and constant. In online journalism, there are special considerations for all these tasks.

No, this chapter's epigraph is *not* suggesting you get drunk before composing your stories—or before doing anything else for that matter. Any veteran of the old newsrooms will quickly tell you the romantic image of the reporter with a bottle of bourbon covering the waterfront and smoking Lucky Strikes is as thin as cheap paint and wears away with the first rain. Real reporters make hay of almost any story thrown their way, rarely suffer from writer's block and can summon up inspiration with a quick walk to the coffeepot.

But the point of composing a story in a rush of energy, insight and single-mindedness is valid, as is the point about bringing a cold, totally impartial and calibrating attitude to the edit.

One of the truly recognizable marks of a professional journalist is the ability to take raw copy (the first rough drafts of the story) and edit it mercilessly. Another is the ability to take even savage editing in stride, with good humor and with a disciplined eye to see what advances the story, not the ego.

In online journalism, once again, the demands are greater than ever, yet the rewards of editing with care are also immeasurably greater.

Seeing the Parts

The first step in editing is to look at all the individual components of the work. Some Silicon Valley managers call it *asset management,* journalists call it knowing the story.

Two parallel tracks are carrying this train to its destination: the journalism of the story and the technology that brings it to the audience. It is important to make sure that the online journalism technology is the right track for getting the reporting to its intended destination.

First and foremost, journalists must consider whether the multimedia tools used advance the story or whether they are there simply because every other story on the site (and perhaps others) uses them.

For example, does the story have a navigation bar—*navbar* in Silicon Valley speak—that stays on one side of the screen through the use of various **frames**? A navbar is currently standard issue, whether it helps the story and site or not. Anyone who has been online for more than 10 minutes has seen a navbar or two. They are typically on the left side of the screen and take up about 20 percent of the total screen size. They serve as a sort of table of contents with links to chapters. The viewer clicks on the link to the desired chapter and the chapter pops up on the main part of the screen (the 80 percent on the right side). The navbar remains the same.

The idea behind the navbar appeals to the traditional newspaper journalist: jam lots of news into a small space. (Online people tend to use the odious word *content*—odious because *content* can also mean stuffing in a pillow, cellulose in dog food and air in a balloon. Journalists are not in the content business. They are in the news business. News is a quality product not to be confused with the implicit, generic message *content* delivers. And top-shelf journalism is identified by precision, not by generic terms and definitions.)

But the standard navbars of so many news sites may actually do damage to a story. Here's how:

- *There is only a small amount of room on the computer screen.*
  Most people have computers designed for monitors no more than 11 by 8 inches. That's very small. Most television screens are far larger (a standard 27-inch screen measures 22 by 16 inches). A standard newspaper page is about 22 by 13.5 inches. On the Web there is even less space available because of the border the browser places around the screen (called "the chrome" by Web authors). The navbar takes about an inch off the top and probably an inch or two off the side so there is even less room for the story. For those with newspaper backgrounds, this is the equivalent of reducing the **news hole** by 10 percent or more; from a broadcast perspective, this is 24 seconds cut from a 120-second story. From a more universal point of view, this is a strip of land cut from the borders of a home owner's lot.

- *The viewer's eye will have to fight another element in trying to find focus.*
  The storyteller is about to tell the story, but the listener is hearing other noises, if faint, saying there is something else worth listening to.

- *The site will look like every other unimaginative Web site online.*
  This is a signal to the audience that the site has no special identity, nothing special to offer and will prompt people to leave it.

  If possible, you should consider avoiding navbars in your stories and if you feel you have to use navbars, you should look for new ways to lay out the page so that the navbar adds to the story line rather than detracting from it.

Another major consideration is whether to **scroll** down the page to see it all. This is a common question in Web circles: to scroll or not to scroll. This issue is by no means settled. Online writers everywhere ceaselessly debate the merits of scrolling down a story versus clicking through to another page. Both sides have much to recommend their methods. However, since, as author Martha Sammons states, "Web readers don't like scrolling," it is generally better *not* to scroll, but to organize the story into pages that compel people to go on to the next link, whatever it may be. The reason is fairly simple. Either action is going to require the audience to use the mouse or a button or another tool to go on, but unless it has a specific purpose, such as revealing something deliberately hidden below the initial bottom of the page, the scroll is likely to be unattractive to the audience. It may be that scrolling feels more like **page jumps** in a newspaper, and studies have proved time and time again that most newspaper readers stop reading stories at the jump. Of course, compelling links have some of the same quality, but they are also gateways to the power of the Web.

The same sort of rigorous questions must be asked for all the elements in your stories, from the layout, to the font, to the length of the audio. Why is it done this way? What is the real message? Does the element move the story forward or is it simply a diversion that seemed like a good idea at the time? Or—and this is one of the most common sins—is the element there just to show off your technical skills?

■ Ethics in Online Journalism

Almost every decision in journalism has an ethical component. Like so many other topics in online journalism, the topic of ethics sparks deep discussions, as well it should. Although you must consider ethics in making decisions throughout the news-gathering process, the beginning of the final assembly is an appropriate time to review the whole picture from an ethical standpoint.

Many primary ethical considerations revolve around a topic addressed in some depth in Chapter 3: advertising. For commercial sites, questions about the role of advertisements are especially relevant. Some of these questions are:

■ *Should there be links to advertisers in news stories?*
For all practical purposes, the answer to this question is already in: There is no choice. Ads in stories *must* be clearly defined as ads and *must* be distinct from news, but those ads will have to serve as a link

or the advertiser will not participate. The great pressure facing commercial news sites is the *click-through rate* on ads. In other words, the advertiser determines how much to pay for an ad by the number of people who click on it, taking the viewer away from the news site and to the advertiser's site. Even worse for online journalists, advertisers want their ads to use the best multimedia technology to attract the audience, and this technology is time-consuming to build, slow to download and distracting when it appears.

■ *Should news sites accept expensive new technology in return for favorable ad placement?*
Such arrangements can be extremely seductive, but they also say, very clearly, that the journalist can be bought. One high-tech company routinely offers major news and information sites high-end equipment with the proviso that those sites can be viewed only with the company's products. Journalists with integrity have said "no, thank you." People without integrity posing as journalists have said yes, and in that instant have said no to their audience, which can never trust them again to report without fear or favor.

■ *Should news sites allow company logos in news stories?*
No. These are ads, plain and simple. Company logos *must not* be in the body of any story. Including a company logo is like putting a story before the world with a For Sale sign.

Many of the most credible American journalists are dealing with these issues in great depth and with great agony. Since the rise of the popular press 20 years before the Civil War, the press has survived and then prospered mightily from advertising revenue. That will not change. What could change is the party in control of a free press: the advertiser or the journalist. Hitching any part of a news product directly to the desires of an advertiser is anathema to a real reporter.

Although the lure of money and getting something for free is powerful, it is by no means the only temptation online journalists face. Among the many essential issues of ethics in online journalism are others that were previously addressed, such as altering digitized photos and corrections. The pioneer journalists of the 21st century will continue to face tough decisions in all these areas.

Over many years a code of ethics has evolved from traditional news outlets; most of it is directly applicable to online news. The San Antonio

Many good local news organizations are marked by their attention to ethics. The San Antonio Express-News proves that you don't have to be the New York Times or the Chicago Tribune to spend time and attention on ethics. All journalists, regardless of medium, need to define and practice an ethical code of behavior.

Reprinted with permission. Copyright © 2000 by San Antonio Express-News.

Express-News has put together one of the best lists of ethical concerns and rules available on the Web (http://www.expressnews/comaboutus/ethics.shtml). We recommend you take time to look at it in depth. The code of conduct is broadly summarized here:

- The company should pay your way for tickets, meals, merchandise. Do not accept gifts from sources or potential sources.

- Don't drink alcohol when covering an event, even if you are covering an event where drinks are free or there is a no-host bar.

- Always identify yourself as a working journalist *before* you begin to work. Information gathered before this is done may be unusable. The only exception is in the case of an undercover investigation. But that technique is almost never needed. Undercover work is almost always a gimmick or shortcut and is an open invitation to lawyers to sue for fraud or invasion of privacy.

- The *appearance* of a conflict of interest is as harmful as an actual conflict of interest. Serious journalists do not even put bumper stickers on their cars.

- Public appearances on behalf of the company should not result in any personal gain for you.

The Society of Professional Journalists has a well-regarded Web site on journalism ethics (http://www.spj.org/ethics/index.htm). Refer to it in matters of doubt, knowing that doubt is a good and healthy sign. In addition, the American Society of Newspaper Editors sponsors a Journalism Values Institute, which published a good paperback on journalism ethics. This book is available online at http://www.asne.org/kiosk/publist.htm.

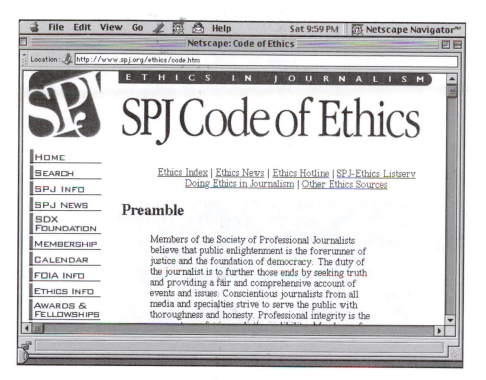

The Society of Professional Journalists has an excellent online site for ethics at http://www.spj.org/ethics/code.htm.

Used with the permission of the Society of Professional Journalists.

Seeing the Whole

After looking over some of the basic parts of a story, it is imperative for you to look again at the whole story. The best way to do that is to run through as if it were any other site on the Web. What is attention grabbing? What isn't? What is the story really saying? What is clear? What is confusing?

The next step is to find some people who know nothing about your story, plant them in front of a screen and ask them to take a look. Step out of view, watch and takes notes about where they put the **cursor,** where they stop and spend time, what they skip over, where they get lost. A fancy term for this is *usability testing.* It's really not much more than a basic road test. Doing this with no more than three people will provide an excellent starting point from which to make the first big edit.

Some of the key questions to ask these auditors when they are done are:

- What is the one lasting point of the story you will take home with you?
- What mood has the story left you with?
- Were people harmed or treated unfairly by the story? Did they have a chance to respond?
- What was the most confusing part of the story?
- Did you want a better or clearer idea where to go in the story? Did you want more freedom of choice in moving about?
- Would you bookmark the story? Why or why not?

There are no rules governing the length of any story. Our feature-length stories on Newsport tend naturally to run 10 to 20 documents, or pages (or screens). But not always. If a story runs long, it must be tight enough to sustain the audience's interest throughout. Viewers may want to bookmark the site (or mark it as a favorite in Microsoft's Internet Explorer Internet browser) if the story is too large for them to go through all at once, which is fine. Chapter 1 discussed using three tiers in stories. This model or a model like it can also be used to offer the audience more choices.

Laurie Kretchmar, editor in chief of Women.com, has a very practical checklist for online journalists:

- *Think like Walt . . . (as in Walt Disney).*
  Aim for an immersive experience, a Main Street USA or Space Mountain. The goal: to be as informative and, yes, entertaining as possible.

- *Pick a great team.*
  Producing a piece for the Net is a collaborative effort. One of the most crucial team members is the artist or designer who can make the difference between an okay-looking piece and a terrific, eye-catching one. Be or draft a good designer to work with you, to craft a logo, to lay out the page or, if you're doing everything yourself, to give you a few pointers.

- *Be flexible.*
  Brainstorm different ways to approach your package. Go for some zany ones. Get your teammates to throw out ideas. You might come up with something totally unique.

■ *Be nice to your audience.*

Aim for easy-to-load pages with no more than 50K of information per page, which includes copy, images and even ads if your site serves up advertisements. Any more and you're being cruel to your audience. Also, be thoughtful. Use simple, clear explanations if you're telling people how to download a **plug-in;** fill out "alt" HTML tags with short descriptions so people with slower-loading Internet connections or those with images turned off can find out what you're envisioning. Double-check all links to other Web pages or sites to make sure they work.

■ *Think nonlinear.*

Your package may have a beginning, middle and end to you, but lay it out and think of it in chunks so that interested viewers can jump right to the sections that appeal to them and don't have to go page by page.

■ *Think, "Then what?"*

Once someone's checked out your great piece, ask yourself, "Then what?" What do you want the person to do? How can you involve the audience in a way that makes sense? Marketing folks call this kind of behind-the-scenes thinking "the call to action." Would you like to invite your audience to e-mail you with feedback? Share stories in a nearby message-board forum? Write letters (e-mail ones, of course) to Congress? Send in JPEGs of themselves? Think of a way to involve your audience and build it in from the start.

■ *Think big.*

In thinking big and bold, think beyond whether it could win you an award. Think about this: Could your package work in other mediums? Could it be translated to TV? To radio? To print? What would you need to do to modify it?

■ *Go for quality.*

Serve your audience. Aim for great, snappy headlines, smart links, no typos, no broken GIFs, video clips that enhance your story. That type of care and craftsmanship could even get you a job. Even if you never hear about it, your audience will appreciate it.

■ Another Word About Links

It is important to avoid putting links in a story that take the audience away from the story itself—or from the overall site. A separate page at the end of a story, called a *source page,* can provide all the links to other Web sites that have additional material.

For example, a story about AIDS may have a link to the Centers for Disease Control (http://www.cdc.gov)—but at the end of the piece, *not* where the agency is cited in the story. The reasons behind this tactic are relatively straightforward. First, journalists worked hard to get your story, and you are proud of that work. It doesn't make sense to devote that sort of care and attention to the story and then give people an easy opportunity to ignore it. Second, from a purely commercial standpoint, you don't want to lose **page views,** the all-important measure of readership that will determine whether advertisers will buy space (making it possible for you to get paid on Friday so you can eat on Saturday).

◼ Rewriting, Reshooting, Redrawing, Rescripting

Editing can be a test of your professional resolve. In the process, you will almost certainly have to rewrite a good deal of your copy. You will have to get new images, either shot by yourself or found legally in other media. You will most likely have to go into software programs such as Photoshop and Illustrator and redraw for clarity. And if the piece is truly interactive, you will find flaws and will have to rescript some coding.

A primary problem encountered is inattention to file sizes. No more than 50 kilobytes should weigh down a page (1K is the equivalent in digital data of about one page of double-spaced text. 1K is about 1,000 bytes. A byte is 8 bits. A bit is the smallest measurable amount of data on the computer. A megabyte is just over 1 million bytes. A gigabyte is just over 1 billion bytes. And, since we're at it, a terabyte is about a trillion bytes.) With graphics, sound files and goodness knows what else that number can soar quickly. The rule of thumb for reducing the file size of graphics is to reduce the size, color intensity and resolution to just below the acceptable level (determined by your subjective eye) and then to raise the quality a notch or two just to the level of acceptability.

How will you know if your readers will have to wait too long for a story to download? Looking carefully at your own work or grabbing a stranger, a cousin or roommate to do so is a start, but hardly a finish if you plan on becoming a real reporter. Real reporters have editors and producers for true quality assurance. In small news organizations, reporters sometimes turn to each other for this role, a poor but better-than-nothing solution.

Another common error is not being particularly attentive to typos, misspellings and syntactical errors. Using the spellchecker in a word processing program will solve only some of the problem. There are hundreds of jokes about Web sites that look ridiculous after the text has been run through a spell-check program. For example, "He rote everything and eight everything two know thee affects," is correct according to a spellchecker. Similarly, grammar and syntax checks should be used with caution. They inevitably suggest rewrites that would be incorrect. Journalists need to know their language as well as their culture.

It is commonly asked by pros how anyone can call himself or herself a real journalist if they haven't got an editor. The best editor is someone who has professional editing experience and who understands what it takes to report the story, tell the story and tell the story in an online medium. These skills are rare, but vital to the creation of a site with value.

Here is a brief example of how a seemingly strong first draft of a news feature story about the big business of strip clubs was substantially rewritten for the Web. The student's long copy had to be made far leaner for the online news site. (The real names of the workers and corporation have been removed.)

Original copy

John Jones is the head of XXX security for the San Francisco XXX-owned and operated clubs. He has a few security guards that work under him, but a bulk of the work falls to John. For two years he has spent five days a week patrolling the XXX clubs, making sure that trouble stays away from the door.

John likes his job because it gives him freedom to move about from club to club, instead of being stuck behind the desk. John is less enthusiastic about the 8pm–3am shift which keeps him away from his wife during the night, and sleeping most of the day away.

Security for XXX is really no different than for any other nightclubs. The customers are for the most part well behaved, the problems arise when someone has a little too much to drink. In the event of a problem John is always nearby, as all of the XXX clubs that he works for are within a two blocks of each other.

John is an employee of XXX corporation, but like many employees he doesn't receive benefits. The benefits, as John sees it, are that he is free to roam between the clubs, and of course, the women. John admits that there are few jobs where one is paid, and gets in free to see women strip.

His relationship to the managers of the clubs is relaxed and respectful. Because John is security at all of the clubs he doesn't have to answer to any specific manager, he receives his orders from the district managers, and his paycheck from XXX corporation.

John doesn't always agree with how the clubs are run, but he realizes he is security, not management, so he just tries to do his job well. He has never had any problems with how he is treated by XXX, and intends to continue working for the corporation in his current job.

Rewritten copy

John Jones heads the small XXX security detail for the San Francisco XXX-owned and operated clubs. For two years he's made sure trouble stays away from the door.

John says he likes the freedom to move about from club to club, instead of being stuck behind the desk. John is less enthusiastic about the 8pm–3am shift.

Security for XXX is typical for most clubs. According to John, the customers are for the most part well behaved. Problems arise when someone has a little too much to drink. John is an employee of XXX corporation, but like many employees he doesn't receive benefits. The benefits, as John sees them, include the freedom to roam between clubs—and then, of course, there are the women. John says there are few jobs where one can receive a paycheck and see women strip.

John Jones says he has never had any problems with how he is treated by XXX, and intends to continue working for the corporation.

The copy was shortened from 320 to 132 words, although the meaning and the essential style of the original remain. Although this example does not take facts and figures and break them into bulleted or numbered lists (a technique demonstrated throughout this book), it does show how much leaner the copy could become and without giving up the essential points the producers felt had to be made with words. Other information was displayed in the site through photos, graphics and animation (http://NewsPort.sfsu.edu/archive/s99/strip/).

The people who will define the future of news and information are the students of today who will be the reporters, editors and producers of tomorrow and the publishers of the not-too-distant future. These people will truly shape the wild days ahead. They will require the discipline of strong editing and in turn will be able to teach it to others. Editing is a critical last safety check before the crucial next phase: publication.

Five Hot Tips for Successful Online Journalists (or How to Deal With the 26-Year-Old Harvard M.B.A. Who'd Rather You Didn't Exist)

RICHARD GINGRAS

Nothing about the Web is automatically the same as what came before. Nothing. Not the technology, not the way products are marketed to us nor the way we buy them, not the way we communicate with one another, not the way we write, not the way we think.

It can be said without hyperbole that the Internet is causing no less than a complete rebuilding of our civilization's central nervous system. And as the rewiring proceeds, new media forms and new media businesses will continue to be generated.

Every new medium develops its own set of standards and practices, from policies that guide editorial decisions to parameters on the sale and placement of advertising. In its earliest days, television transmitted a strikingly clear message that its content policies did not derive from the newspapers of the day—the persistent Camel cigarette backdrop on NBC's first network news program, the "Camel News Caravan," for example.

Although television news behaviors have moderated over time, they are still significantly different from those of newpapers—note the quirky ritual of an ABC sports anchor interviewing a Toyota marketing vice president at the close of a sponsored golf event. And many newspapers with distinguished histories don't always clearly communicate the raison d'être of a piece of published content—consider the pseudo-editorial of special newspaper sections on autos, gardening or other topics of interest to advertisers. Protests that they are clearly labeled are usually lame.

The evolving Web takes the notion of change to the extreme. Nearly its entire foundation is resting on the fractured remains of broken traditions. There is no aspect of communications, media, technology, or business that is not being scrutinized by savvy entrepreneurs looking for a way to break the model and grab a market from a deeply entrenched company. The success of Amazon and a hundred others has only reaffirmed to every entrepreneur that success comes from breaking rules, not from respecting them. Tradition is meaningless to the newly spawned M.B.A. driven to make a hundred million dollars by the age of 30. Tradition, by their thinking, is roadkill.

Today there is a nascent struggle on the Web to define and re-define the way content and advertising relate. Three key characteristics are apparent. First, the online medium will be extremely different and varied, as nearly anyone can easily create and distribute content (advertisers, publishers, individuals). Second, these myriad content offerings can so easily be linked together (review the book, buy the book) that each component of content begs for its own labeling and sourcing. Third, the M.B.A.-schooled entrepreneurs driving Web development know little of traditional media ethics and will aggressively challenge any assumption that these ethics should be carried to the Web.

An online journalist cannot avoid participating in the creation of what will ultimately become the Web's traditional standards and practices. Doing and saying nothing has its own impact. Reporters, editors and producers have to deal with standards, struggle with them and try to shove them one more inch in the right direction. Here are five things the online journalist should think about in fighting the good fight.

1. *Talk about the value of trust.*

   Never say, "This is the way journalists/editors/producers have always done it." Not even once. Do so and you'll lose credibility: "You don't get it," will be the dismissive response.

   Your compatriots on the business side don't know, don't understand, don't care about traditional standards and practices. What they do care about is the success of their business model. Regularly point out that visitors who do not trust editorial content will not provide the usage and loyalty the business plan requires. Preach the value of credibility, quality and trust *because* they are good for business.

2. *Know your ethics and strive to practice them visibly.*

   In traditional media, standards and practices are typically adhered to by instinct. With a Web publication they must be practiced openly and in a fashion that educates your associates on why ethics are important. Exercise your responsibility to accuracy and quickly correct potentially harmful mistakes with the same volume of the original item. Uncover issues of content labeling, sourcing and conflict of interest and address them in a fashion that communicates why it's important to the business to do so.

3. ***Know the business model as well as the head of marketing does.***
   Editors in traditional media don't think about the business side. They don't feel they should, and indeed they shouldn't have to. On the Web, however, you can't leave it to the business side. You must be an aggressive participant in any dialogue that defines the content business. Take every opportunity to learn the business model, study the supporting spreadsheets, debate the forecasts of page views and visitors and understand the assumptions on audience loyalty (or its reverse, *churn*).

4. ***Define the way content is presented before marketing defines it for you.***
   New methods of presenting editorial content in relation to revenue-driven material—such as close linkage of product-based editorials and product purchases—are inevitable. Be open to exploring new content models and define them before the business side does. Define the appropriate approach to the interface and to the editorial voice. Put the approach in writing, offer it as a possible standard and prepare to defend it.

5. ***Understand your product's usage.***
   No medium before the Web has had such powerful mechanisms for audience measurement. Online journalists can't hide from audience data. Instead, they should own it. Don't resist the analysis. Analyze it. Editors in traditional media have shied away from research and circulation analysis, thinking such practices might interfere with their editorial authority and vision. That's not possible any longer. Use reports on usage to learn about your audience, to refine your product and to satisfy its editorial mission and target circulation.

It's tough to be an editor in this environment. You need to be intellectually sharp and able to speak with great confidence about editorial objectives and values. With that, one bonus tip:

> ***Don't tolerate arrogance from your brethren in traditional media about the comparative qualities of their long-refined editorial product.***

It's debilitating and unnecessary. Traditional print and electronic media products are not as good as they should be. Major newspapers have been living high in one-paper towns and can well benefit from competitive stimulation. And broadcasters with high-quality news products are the exception, not the rule.

In comparison, the Web is an extraordinary publishing medium, one that will foment a more expansive, more inclusive array of journalistic voices than ever before. Most important, this is not a battle between Web-based journalists and traditional media journalists. It's a battle to make sure the Internet evolves with a healthy population of solid editorial products. It's a battle to build a well-understood set of core of journalistic values and Web-appropriate editorial practices that begin to be taken as the norm.

Richard Gingras is senior vice president and general manager of Excite Studios. He was the founding editor in chief and vice president, programming, of the @Home Network. In 1995, while at Apple overseeing the design and programming of the online service eWorld, he arranged the seed financing for Salon.com, the Web's most ambitious foray into original online journalism.

chapter 8

Preparing for Liftoff

Journalism is . . . a rough draft of history that will never be completed about a world we can never understand.
—Philip Graham

Preparing for the publication, or launch, of a Web site and the news stories that will go in it is a little like preparing for Apollo 13—it may seem immensely complicated, exciting and potentially fatal. There is no way to effectively inoculate yourself against the exhilaration or anxiety. But there are ways to manage it all.

The final checks and edits must be dealt with seriously and methodically. Unanticipated problems will arise, and some will appear to be emergencies indeed. But in the end, you will take off into cyberspace, zoom around the world in seconds and bask in the pleasure of great accomplishment. This chapter tells how.

The long days, the moments of despair and the bright hours of triumph come together as you wheel your rocket ship to the launchpad. (*Launching* is the word Silicon Valley masters use when referring to their online sites). The enterprise that is about to be finalized is one you will never forget, especially when the server starts lighting up, signaling that people are looking at your work from computer terminals, PCs, Macs and all sorts of laptops and **PDAs** around the globe. Within minutes, readers may log in from other continents. And your story is likely to prompt e-mail both from around the corner and from other nations.

■ Final Edits

In the final stage, accuracy is most important. Without accuracy, the only meaning the work has is a destructive one. You will, of course, make mistakes. There is not a reporter alive who does not have a nightmare story about making a mistake. Mature, seasoned reporters deal with it. Second-rate, immature and less-than-candid reporters pretend it didn't happen or it wasn't important. Some reporters have escaped punishment for making big mistakes, and others have been pilloried for making relatively inconsequential ones. Like real life, it isn't fair. But that hardly matters.

What matters is developing the mature, professional attitude that you will do everything you can to avoid making mistakes, that when you do make mistakes, they will face those mistakes head-on and that every day they will get better at sensing the danger signs and dealing with them forthrightly. That's what makes a pro.

Factual errors in stories on the World Wide Web have ramifications beyond those in other media. Unlike mistakes made in newspapers, magazines or broadcast stations, errors on the Web are not restricted to a confined circulation area. Instead, they are instantly available to a worldwide audience across the Internet. They may damage lives, enterprises and hopes with equal access by people in Bombay, Buenos Aires and Bangkok, not to mention Providence, Phoenix and Portland. And many people do notice and remark on errors. In fact, there is even a Web site devoted entirely to mistakes made in the news (http://www.slipup.com).

What's more, mistakes may remain on the Web forever. Many sites do not post corrections alongside the original mistake and the file servers keep sending the error out forever. This situation has resulted in a whole set of new problems, which will be examined in the next chapter.

The world of online journalism is less and less forgiving of shoddy practices. Sites such as Slipup.com gleefully troll for mistakes online—and showcase them to the world.

Used with the permission of Slipup.com.

The best way to edit for accuracy is to deconstruct the story point by point. Take each assertion separately and consider:

- How did you come to this conclusion?
- What is the source of the information?
- Is the source solidly reliable?
- Is there at least one other reliable source confirming that assertion?
- Who would dispute the finding? Is the opposing viewpoint being reported?
- If the conclusion were on trial, would a skillful, intelligent and knowledgeable lawyer be able to disprove it?

Going through this type of checklist time and time again will begin to discipline not only the editing, but the reporting and composition as well.

Much of this advice seems directly applicable to the *writing* of a story, and so it is. But in a true multimedia story, which is the goal in online journalism, the information being presented is not restricted to words. Journalists must apply the same sort of checklist to every element used to tell the story.

For example, if photographs are used, were they manipulated in any way? In a well-known case, for the cover of Time magazine a photo editor darkened the picture of O. J. Simpson, former football star turned murder suspect. The editor stated that he made a standard editorial decision to bring a more ominous tone to the cover, signaling the ominous tone of the story inside. Many readers objected, however, seeing a subliminal racism at work, associating dark tones with evil and suggesting that Simpson was guilty although he was legally presumed innocent.

If sound is used in the story is it used to infuse emotion that was not originally there? Is the sound sweetened to give the story more power—or a different sort of power—than it deserves? If sound was removed or not used so as not to clutter up a clear message, was information germane to the story removed also?

For example, an interview conducted on the street might have ambient noise of sirens, horns or yelling, which might make it difficult to hear the interview. But there must have been a reason to conduct the interview there. Perhaps it was part of a story about a beat cop in a sleazy part of the city, in which case the background sound is a true part of the story and the fact that the officer has to yell to be heard adds something to it.

In a moving 1998 Swedish documentary about Asian sweatshops making clothes for European customers, a particularly powerful moment came when whole families, including child laborers, were so exhausted from their work that they lay asleep on the factory floor. In the background the audience could hear John Lennon's "Imagine," a song about his dream for equality and fairness. A reporter asked the story's producer if she had added the sound. She politely said no, it happened to be playing on the radio on the factory floor at the time while the children and parents slept on huge bolts of cloth and piles of European fashions.

◼ Libel

According to the American Heritage Dictionary, libel is "any written, printed, or pictorial statement that damages a person by defaming his character or exposing him to ridicule." Note that the definition does not say that the statement is false, wrong or incorrect. In the courtroom, however, a libel charge will not hold if the information is proved to be accurate. Thus accuracy is not only the prime directive of journalists, but it is also the ultimate defense of a story.

Journalists at times will libel someone according to the dictionary definition. According to the law, though, a story can stand up to a challenge in court if it is defensible. That is, the story must be accurate and without malice. It should be attributed. And it should probably not be about a private citizen who is not a public figure. People who are not in the public eye have stronger rights when prosecuting for libel than do public figures such as celebrities or politicians.

To continue to stress the point made throughout this examination about the vital importance of accuracy, the simple fact is that there is no point to being a journalist if you do not have a well-developed sense of accuracy. Accuracy is far more than protection against lawsuits—it is, again, journalism's prime directive.

Many individuals and companies have abandoned libel claims in favor of other claims that do not protect journalists as well. Fraud has emerged as a favorite grounds for lawsuits. Perhaps the most high-profile case of this instance was a lawsuit brought against ABC News by a major supermarket chain, Food Lion. ABC sent its news personnel to apply for jobs at Food Lion after hearing allegations about the health and safety of the meat sold in the stores. The ABC people lied on their job applications and failed to disclose their employment with the news organization. After they got the jobs, they secretly videotaped health and safety conditions behind the meat counter—conditions that bore out the allegations. But that did not protect ABC.

Food Lion sued, but not initially for libel, although according to Food Lion Spokesperson Tawn Earnest, they filed to do so later and their attempt was rejected. Instead, Food Lion sued ABC News for fraud and a legal term called "breach of the duty of loyalty." And the supermarket chain won in court, though subsequent appeals made the final penalties rather small.

If you have thorny legal questions about a story, consult a lawyer. Students at large universities may find a sympathetic attorney at their affiliated law school. Good journalism schools usually have a media law lawyer who lectures and is available to answer questions on a regular basis. If these options are not available, you may find a lawyer willing to give advice **pro bono.** If all else fails, you must simply get rid of any potentially libelous material in the story.

The large supermarket chain Food Lion sued ABC News in the 1990s after the network broadcast a "20/20" story showing dirty and unsafe conditions in the chain's meat department. Food Lion did not initially contest the truth of the story—which would have gone to the heart of a libel accusation. Instead, Food Lion sued ABC for fraud. Online journalists also have to worry about getting sued for more than libel.

Food Lion logo used with the permission of Food Lion. ABC News logo used courtesy of ABC News.

No serious examination of American journalism can be complete without some discussion of the Bill of Rights. The Constitution of the United States guarantees in its very first amendment the freedom of the press. There are no codicils, no asterisks, no clauses attached. It simply says, "Congress shall make no law . . . abridging the freedom of the press." This

> *Congress shall make no law respecting an establishment of religion, or prohibiting the free exercise thereof; or abridging the freedom of speech, or of the press; or the right of the people peaceably to assemble, and to petition the Government for a redress of grievances.*

The very first item in the Bill of Rights in the Constitution of the United States, the supreme law of the land, guarantees the freedom of the press. It also applies to online journalism.

Courtesy of the National Archives and Records Administration.

is a sacred right that many constitutional scholars argue is the very guarantor of the other rights and freedoms.

There are, of course, other sacred rights, including those that protect the safety of all Americans. In the practice of responsible journalism, there are rarely conflicts among these rights. However, when people post stories and pictures about such topics as child pornography simply to make money and excite prurient interests, they often try to hide under the protection of the First Amendment. This harms everyone. The Bill of Rights must be exercised every day to preserve people's freedom. It is the role of journalists, online and off, to protect First Amendment rights with all the ability they can muster.

Many Web users and authors have been deeply disturbed by attempts to use legitimate concerns about issues such as child pornography on the Net as a censorship tool. Censorship has always been and always will be with us. Its appearance changes from generation to generation and from issue to issue, but there will always be attempts to stop journalists from exercising the right of freedom of the press. But freedom of the press also requires a delicate balancing act, for example, balancing freedom of expression with freedom from the fear of seeing children harmed. The issues are difficult. Online journalists must take their rightful place among journalists of other media and act responsibly, struggle to keep the First Amendment alive and always embrace an honest and lively debate.

"Journalism and democracy share a common fate," wrote Columbia University Graduate School of Journalism Professor James W. Carey. "No journalism, no democracy."

"Journalism can be destroyed by forces other than a totalitarian state," he also warned in an essay about the historic role of journalists. "It can also be destroyed by the entertainment state. When journalists measure their success solely by the size of their readership or audience, by the profits of their companies or by their incomes, status and visibility, they have caved into the temptation of worshipping false gods, of selling their heritage for pottage."

■ Stitching It All Together

In the final stages of the journey toward online publication you must make sure your reporting is right and your technical skills are honed. Here is a checklist:

■ *Layout*
Once again, take a look at the way each document, or page, is laid out. Review the design checklist (Chapter 6). Remember, clarity is key in online design. A cluttered page is a bad page. A page that requires work to understand is a bad page. A page that allows the viewer to grasp the essential news and information easily is a successful page.

- *Navigation*
  Is it easy to get around the page, the story and the site? Is it clear not only what the story is about but also how to get more information else-where on the Web? Anyone who has spent any time on the Web knows the frustration of searching for something hard to find. That is the result of poor navigation and should not happen to your audience.

- *Site structure*
  Directly related to navigation is the structure of the site, or what some Web designers sometimes call information architecture. The site map for the story is the internal road map that guides the audi-ence through it. Check that the audience can go through everything on the site with ease and—at least as important—can get out easily too. Dead ends in Web sites are an open invitation to leave.

- *Browser compatibility*
  There are two dominant Web browsers, Netscape's Navigator and Microsoft's Internet Explorer, and many others, including AOL's browser. A site designed for one browser will not come up in the other the exact same way. You need to test your pages on both Nav-igator and Explorer to make sure the story comes up the way you want it to on both. Most of the time this test will reveal manageable problems that can be fixed by going back into the source code and tweaking a bit.

- *PC and Mac compatibility*
  A similar set of problems can arise when a story is built on a PC and brought up on a Macintosh or the other way around. There are other operating systems as well, such as Linux and Unix, but they remain somewhat specialized and are not used by a mass audience. Although the differences across operating systems may appear small, a story that looks sloppy or unfinished because of incompatibility issues sends a message that the work itself is sloppy—a death sentence for a journalist. And if it crashes someone's computer (this has been known to happen, however infrequently) you will truly have angered the people you should be courting.

- *Compression and quality*
  Review the file size of each page and the various components of each element. Recheck the basic download rates in the chart pro-vided in Chapter 5. Software tools such as DeBabelizer will make compressing big files, including background colors, easier. And

remember, as you slim down your weighty multimedia elements, you will probably denigrate the quality of your graphics. Use your best judgment to decide what is enough and what is too much. Again, the key technique is to keep subtracting from the file size until the result is unacceptable, then to add one step up at a time until you can live with it.

■ *Plug-ins work*
Not all browsers have the ability to read multimedia tools such as Flash or RealPlayer. Doing so requires a plug-in. Viewers usually go to a site on the Internet from which they can download a copy of the plug-in (usually for free). But never take for granted that your audience knows this. Alert your viewers to the need for a plug-in and let them know where to get a copy.

■ *Links*
There is no getting around how important links are to an online news story and news site. This part of the final edit is among the easiest and most important. Simply make sure each and every link actually works. If a link doesn't work, fix it immediately.

■ *Spaces in file names*
A file name is the name of the folder that stores the story's elements—the name to which the links will point. The links will not work if there are spaces or "forbidden" characters—such as #, @, * or even ?—in the filename. Get rid of them. This very common problem can cause major headaches. It should be addressed early on and checked often. If you wait until the end of the process, you'll have a lot of work before you.

■ *Theme, tone and texture*
One last time, with feeling. With smart editors and critical thinking it's always good to stop and remember what the original idea for the story was, what you hoped it would be and how you hoped it would play. Did you accomplish your original aims?

■ *Code*
Finally, print out the **source code** and the text and check everything one last time to be sure it's right. It is easier to proof source code if all the tags are in capital letters, although the actual file names need to be lowercase. Proofing on a screen is tough enough because of screen resolutions, but doing it with material you've been staring at for any length of time is even tougher.

■ Last-Minute Emergencies

This is more of a mental preparation in these early, still wild days of online journalism. Expect that even when the reporting is done, the multimedia authoring complete and the server humming, you will run across unexpected problems. These run the gamut from a complicated code mystery to a software glitch to a hardware meltdown. If you are prepared for something bad to happen, you are more likely to be able to stay cool and levelheaded when it does and to deal with problems professionally. Last-minute emergencies happen. Often. As San Francisco Bay Area Webmaster and journalist Gary Barker puts it: "Every time there's a last minute, there's a last-minute emergency." If everything works out, take it as a good omen and get ready to launch the story onto the World Wide Web.

■ The Launch

The final connection between the story and the server that allows people around the planet to see it is an odd, sometimes unreal and completely prosaic procedure, taking a few minutes of coding, and resulting in wonderment that has few parallels.

If you have your own dedicated server, you make sure all your coding is correct and put the story files in the appropriate directory folder. If you are using a university's server or another server, you may have to use **FTP** to transfer the story to that site, a relatively easy process. All the stories on the news site are connected, then the server is loaded with the data and that's pretty much it. However, because every Web server platform has a different set of instructions, someone who knows how to read a manual and has patience may be needed.

Once you've taken these steps with your story, its launched. You run to another computer down the hall and call up your story and there it is. You call your sister across the country and give her the URL, she calls it up on her terminal at work and she sees pretty much what you see. Your father overseas gets your e-mail with the Web address and he sees it in an instant. You go home and try it in the middle of the night and marvel at the beauty, the power and elegance of the central circuit board connecting us all.

This is a time when you will experience hope and not a little anxiety. But if you have done everything you were supposed to, the anxiety is unfounded.

It's All About Invention

RUSTY COATS

Launching a Web site from scratch, remastering a site from the inside out, transitioning a staff of start-up pioneers to seasoned professionals, forging partnerships with competitors and engaging in fistfights with new enemies—going online did something marvelous and terrifying to the journalism industry. It forced journalists to reinvent themselves in ways that would have sent them screaming into the streets only a decade ago.

I launched ModBee.com—the Web site of the Modesto (California) Bee—in 1996 with the help of a programmer. Together we wrote a publishing tool to back-end with our newsroom system, designed a site, identified new content and set up a continuous news cycle for feeding it. From the moment I was named online news manager to our launch six weeks later, we were asking fundamental questions about our identity and role. What does metro mean online? What does breaking news mean? How do we handle open reader forums after traditionally screening the opinions of our readers? How will we react when we learn that sports is the most popular section—and sports is less popular than our classified ads? And how do we keep our new product afloat with a staff of one?

In 1996, none of us had answers. One could argue we still don't. What we did know was that we had to reinvent how we viewed ourselves and what we would accomplish. And that after the heroism of launching a Web site, we knew that the process was only beginning.

I moved to Sacramento in 1997 to manage the staff at sacbee.com, the Web site for the Sacramento (California) Bee. The site had been online for six months and was beginning to suffer under its own weight, as all sites do, because the content had grown beyond its original structure. (When was the last time a newspaper could make that complaint?) The expectation and sophistication of our users had ballooned. Online, the bar isn't rising—it's rocketing. Readers wanted customization and e-mail products and better searchability and the ability to e-mail stories to friends. So we gutted the site and restructured it, one phase at a time, reinventing a site that was less than a year old.

We did that twice in the two years I was there. We simply couldn't change fast enough. No one in this game can. We're new to change. Media companies aren't accustomed to redefining work flow and brand and scope in the space of a few weeks. It traditionally takes months of process before media companies will even consider changing a masthead font.

Online, you need to do that in a day. Or less. Because the target—the market, users and even goals—is Dopplering away from you and you need to step on the gas. So you have to embrace your enemies—TV, radio and newspaper companies—to create regional portals, a one-stop-shopping destination, hoping to attract more viewers. Former competitors become allies against larger enemies—from Yahoo! to MSNBC, brands that didn't exist 10 years ago—who attract far more local viewers than do media companies. These new competitors, untethered by the baggage of 150-year processes, move at a blurred pace, which—along with the lure of stock options and a less traditional workplace—lure our best people away.

And so we churn staff. There are darned few launch pioneers in the online media world who haven't left the industry. It's as if the process of invention genetically altered the media pioneers; once they embraced change and digital delivery, they couldn't stop. And few media companies change fast enough. It's an old saying: The colonists on the second boat never found the colonists on the first. That's because the first wave had already moved over the next hill.

We're building news reports tailored for cellular phones and wireless palm computers. Print newsrooms are creating radio shows for Real-Audio players and TV news shows for Webcasts. TV stations are writing print stories for their Web sites. Magazines such as Fast Company are creating regional community groups through online discussion groups. We're using new muscles—usually before we've had time to develop them fully, simply because the Internet demands that we learn as we do. Or, as has become the motto of online media: Ready, fire, aim.

Ten years ago, we couldn't have imagined the aggressive news cycles the Internet demands nor the skills required to produce competitive Web sites and wireless channels. We couldn't have imagined partnering with our competition or creating front pages featuring more commerce-oriented services than headlines. Ten years ago, we were still gazing at our navels—wondering about the usefulness of color graphics and fretting about the USA Todaying of our sacred product.

We couldn't imagine reinventing ourselves. Again and again and again.

Rusty Coats is online editor of startribune.com, the Web site for The Star Tribune in Minneapolis. Previous to that he was online content manager at sacbee.com, the Web site of The Sacramento Bee, and online news manager of modbee.com, the Web site of The Modesto Bee. He worked as a reporter and columnist before moving online.

chapter 9

A Journalist's Introduction to Online Intellectual Property

*Where the press is filled with good news, one can be
pretty sure that the jails are filled with good men.*
—Daniel Patrick Moynihan

The online journalist faces more challenges than those presented by Web authoring and reporting in a totally new media environment. Some laws that have governed journalism are now turned on their sides in the enterprise ahead. Most crucial for all online journalists is the need to appreciate the vast changes in a field that was once a peripheral issue: copyright law.

There has rarely been so much turbulence in such a short period of time, but it is natural considering all the froth churned up by the powerful new technologies. In the interest of helping you avoid pain and cost, this chapter will review the changes and rules that apply to the new world of online journalism.

The struggle to win a free press, the essential component for a free people, is never over. The enemy of a free press and of a free people changes his face, his voice, his many disguises—but he is always with us. Americans at the beginning of the 21st century are particularly lucky in the history of this struggle because some of the rules that might seem to fence them in also serve to protect them.

The rules are always shifting somewhat, but rarely do they shift as dramatically as they have with the advent of the Internet and of the World Wide Web in particular. The Internet has prompted deep fault-line shifts in copyright law.

■ Copyright Law

Not so long ago when people went to browse for news and information they went down to the local newsstand, where the smell of ink mixed with old cigars and newsprint. Browsing today more often means getting on the Web and clicking hyperlinks looking for news, information and amusement.

In the old way of browsing, if people wanted a picture in a magazine, a story in a newspaper, a chart in a book, they bought the item from the shopkeeper behind the counter. The shopkeeper used the money to pay for living expenses—groceries, rent—and to pay the person who delivered the material to the shop.

Today, the friendly shopkeeper behind the newsstand counter and the nice salesperson who delivered the papers, magazines and books are out of a job. Maybe now they're taking classes on how to write in HTML and edit using Photoshop. (The landlord of the building where the newsstand used to be is happy with the new tenant, Starbucks.) And today, people browsing the Web can simply copy the picture or the text or anything else posted with a click or two of the mouse. No charge.

Does that mean people can copy anything and use it for free? Hardly. The revolution in the ease of use of copying materials has refocused attention on copyright laws with the sort of intensity unseen for decades.

U.S. copyright laws can be traced to England in 1710. The Statute of Anne was the first national copyright law and the model for the first legislation in the United States in 1790. It has since expanded across the world and been seriously rebuilt in the United States as late as 1998, with the passage of the Digital Millennium Copyright Act.

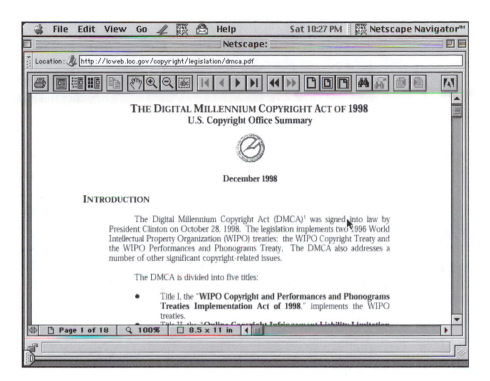

The Digital Millennium Copyright Act represents the biggest changes in copyright law in a century and was brought about chiefly because of the new challenges introduced to communications by the Internet.

The law today says:

- *Copyright laws immediately protect virtually every sort of "expression" that is fixed in a tangible form.*
  That means any literary, dramatic, musical, pictorial, sculptural or architectural expression. It also means the moment the words or pictures or sounds produced on a computer are **saved to disk,** they are protected.

- *The definition of what is expression is vast.*
  E-mail is protected, a posting in a newsgroup or listserv is protected, as is the photo of the dog posted on someone's home page.

- *The protections last for years.*
  If the work was published before 1978, the copyright lasts at least 75 years and could last longer if renewed. If the work was created, but

not published, before 1978, the copyright expires at the end of the year 2002. If the work was created after 1978 and is owned by an individual, it is protected for the life of the author plus 50 years. If it was created after 1978 and is owned by an employer of the author, the copyright's life span is 75 years from the original date of publication or 100 years from the date of creation, whichever happens first.

■ *Take heart, not everything is copyrighted.*
Although the expression of an idea, a fact or a title is protected, the actual idea, fact or title is not. For example, the local newspaper may have done a story about telephone answering machines interfering with direct communication between people. That story is protected by copyright. But the story idea is not. For that reason alone (not to mention the poor quality of some work in the journalism industry) the same story ideas are repackaged, rewritten and, in the argot of the new media, "repurposed" over and over again (a fact that is hardly lost on readers, viewers and users of news, who turn elsewhere after a while).

There is one more exception to copyright law that is of major importance to all journalists: a provision known by lawyers as Fair Use.

■ Fair Use

It is fair and legal to use copyrighted materials for these specific purposes:

- ■ Research
- ■ Teaching
- ■ Library Activities
- ■ Parody
- ■ Criticism
- ■ Journalism

It is this last exemption, naturally, in which journalists are most interested.

Let's say you are doing a story about the Rolling Stones' successful concert tours and you want to use their music to liven up your site—that's a copyright infringement. But if in your story you point out that the band began with "Start Me Up," using a portion of the song is legal and you are probably legally protected. You may use only enough (less than five seconds), though, to make your point.

Perhaps you are doing a story about how the turn of the millennium was a major business opportunity for many people. You may want to use the very overused song "1999" by the musician from Minneapolis who changes his name as often as Michael Jackson changes his face. If you use part of the song only, and use it as an example of how money was made by people celebrating the millennium, you are probably protected and legally shielded by the doctrine of Fair Use. Again, use only enough (that's right, less than five seconds) to make your point. Music is one of the most fiercely protected forms of expression in the world. And some media companies are especially vigilant in protecting their property and will aggressively attack with lawyers (Disney comes to mind first).

Regardless of the nature of the company or the type of intellectual property involved, real reporters will always respect the rights of intellectual property, much as they want people to respect their ownership of their stories.

Some of the other Fair Use provisions often applicable to journalists are parody and criticism. For example, columnists would be unable to do their work if they couldn't make fun of Mick Jagger or Mickey Mouse. Nonetheless, good taste and good thinking will help protect you, your story and your site.

There is a great deal at stake for both sides. For you, there is your livelihood, reputation and future. For intellectual property owners, there is the same. By the end of the 20th century the core copyright businesses—publishing, film and music—were doing well over $200 billion in business each year. They have no intention of giving away any part of those stakes and will pay many lawyers for many hours to defend their rights. In addition, Web technologies, such as **spiders,** automatically and ceaselessly search the Web looking for intellectual property theft and report back to their masters.

You will want to defend your rights as well. The Web leaves all creators of original expressions open to theft as never before. One of the biggest battles already engaging reporters is a nasty habit picked up by some Web site managers who make reference to a news story, thinking it will exempt them through fair use, and then place it in a frame inside their own site. A site called TotalNEWS (http://totalnews.com) was among the first to get caught doing this, angering major players such as the Wall Street Journal, Time Warner and Reuters. The parties settled out of court in 1997, with TotalNEWS agreeing to stop the practice, but the courts never had a chance to rule on the case, leaving the real battle for sometime in the future. If TotalNEWS had used only small excerpts from the stories, had attributed those excerpts *and* had had links back to the original sites, the lawyers probably would not have appeared.

In another celebrated case, the ClariNet site (http://www.clarinet. com) paid the giant Knight Ridder news company for using humorist Dave Barry's column. But someone on the Usenet portion of the Internet, where most newsgroups live, had less respect for the property of others and used Barry's original and expressions without permission. Knight Ridder responded by pulling Barry's work off ClariNet, a loss to everyone.

■ Trademarks and Soundmarks

Copyright is not to be confused with trademarks. A trademark can be any word, name, symbol or device used to identify a product, company or individual. For example, the white swirls on a red can of Coca-Cola are trademarked symbols of Coke. So are the names Coca-Cola and Coke. So are old advertising slogans such as "Sign of Good Taste." The list goes on and on.

The number of trademarks often flabbergasts novice reporters. You can be sure if you post or publish a story about Realtors and do not capitalize the R, you will get a notice from a local Realtor letting you know it is a trademarked term and may be used only if spelled correctly. (Some reporters use the term *real estate agent* instead, just to get around what smells like a cheap advertising issue.) Other common trademarked words include Jell-O, Kleenex and Xerox.

Trademarks, as a reflection of a growing multimedia world, are expanding to other areas of mass communication. Soundmarks are now increasingly common, with companies signature audio. For instance, AT&T has soundmarked the ring callers hear just before a long-distance call is processed. NBC's chimes are also soundmarked.

Online journalists should be careful when using words, symbols or even sounds, which may be trademarks. For example, Kleenex is a registered trademark for a variety of products, not a generic term for facial tissue.

Used with the permission of the Kimberly-Clark Corporation. Kleenex is a registered trademark of Kimberly-Clark Corporation.

Be careful of using trademarks, soundmarks and other proprietary symbols in your news stories, unless you have a good reason to use them. The rules of Fair Use are in play here as well, but so is good judgment.

■ Copyright Checklist

Some of the basic questions you must ask yourself before using someone else's work are:

- Is this person's work necessary to tell the story and is it actually part of the story?
- Does the story use just enough to make its point, or does it use more than is really necessary?
- Is the material being used in a way that will allow others to use it without going to the owner for permission?
- Is the product or reputation of the owner being damaged in any way? If so, is it being done for a clear, reasonable purpose?
- Does the use expose you or your colleagues, friends, or family to any harm, financial or otherwise?

When you can answer these questions with comfort, you are heading in the right direction: toward real journalism.

The New Information Railroad

JAMES WHEATON

In the Digital Age, old laws meet new technologies and the likely result appears to be a train wreck. The only question is, How do we avoid one?

The oft-heard cry of the Internet is "Information wants to be free!" Nonsense.

Information doesn't want anything. People want information to be free. Free in the economic as well as in the philosophical sense. But what is truly free information? Is it the notion that all information is part of the Zeitgeist, the collective knowledge of humankind, and the lucky person who publishes it has no claim to own it? Is it the related notion that any idea, expression or thought becomes part of the public endowment upon publication so that in putting their thoughts out there, people give up control?

Some of the evolving culture of the Internet, particularly the libertarian strain that runs through many Netizens, adheres to some or all of this formulation.

Such a regime has been tried, once, in human history. In revolutionary France the reaction to the destruction of the monarchy's absolute monopoly on what could be printed was to replace it with its opposite; no one owned any expression. The result? Printers and publishers simply stopped paying for any content and started copying anything that sold. And there was a race to the bottom.

But we live in an age in which content is the new king, its controllers the new royalty. In this world information will not be free.

That said, the economic forces that have resulted in enormous conglomerations of capital in media, with an increasingly small number of large players controlling media content, have also given rise to increasing political power. That power is being expressed in every venue where control of content is being discussed:

■ In local communities, where local governments no longer want to grant public access to public information gathered and maintained at public expense, often gathered under compulsion of law, preferring instead to sell or lease it, often at exorbitant cost or through exclusive contracts with private providers

- In statehouses, where laws are proposed to grant new rights to prevent content that huge media celebrities don't want (for example, people like Woody Allen might not be eager to see their private lives splashed all over the media, new or old)

- In Washington, D.C., where the subcommittees and working groups of the Information Infrastructure Task Force, created by President Clinton in 1993 to implement a new National Information Infrastructure, have a strong bias toward resolving issues solely on the basis of what will enhance commerce, that is, money-based interests

- In Switzerland, where the World Intellectual Property Organization, often led by shrill demands from U.S. representatives, has seriously considered granting intellectual property status to every single item in electronic databases

Common in all these forums is that the people who should care the most—writers and their readers—are absent. Therefore, information cannot be free, nor can the rules for its costs and control be left to those whose sole measure of interest is how much money can be made from the information.

As James Madison noted in the Federalist Papers over two hundred years ago, "Knowledge will forever govern ignorance and a people who mean to be their own governors must arm themselves with the power knowledge gives. A popular government without popular information or the means of acquiring it is but a prologue to a farce or tragedy or perhaps both."

Copyright is always a balance between protecting the private interest of those who create content to be able to profit from their labors and protecting the public interest by ensuring that information, ideas and thoughts enrich all and not just a few. That balance will not be finally struck online anymore than off it, but the formerly anarchic Web is quickly being brought to ground.

In the end, copyright rules designed for a world of paper and ink will probably also work for one of bits and bytes. The following are some observations to help the budding journalist in an unfamiliar world.

1. Does copyright even apply in cyberspace?

Unquestionably. Only the fool thinks otherwise. But copying on the Web is so easy, so quick, so surreptitious that it almost feels as if doing it is all right. It's true that the Web is different from paper. You access a book, magazine or newspaper without copying any of it, but you can't access a Web site without making a copy of it, at least to your RAM and your cache. But is it okay to save what you copy to your hard drive?

Those who control content are trying to say no. They will lose. A single copy on your own hard drive will remain fair use just as your videotaped copy of the "Movie of the Week" off the television is okay. But you shouldn't reproduce that stored Web page and distribute copies to your friends, colleagues, clients or customers, just as you shouldn't copy that VCR tape or charge your friends admission to watch it.

2. Fair Use.

The rules of fair use will continue to hold online, so the careful journalist needs to remember the same basic rules for determining what is fair and what is not in the journalistic sense.

Query: Is the material you are copying in some way the subject of the article, or are you doing it to dress up your piece on some other topic?

Query: How much of the material are you copying—just enough to explain, or so much that the reader needn't bother going to the site you plundered?

Query: Can your work stand without the copied material?

3. Web Design.

Design is content, every bit as much as words and pictures.

4. Web Links and Windows.

The world of the Web and links raises many questions for online publishers and many are without clear answers.

Can you link to another person's site without that person's permission? The legal answer coming back is yes, but Netiquette says take it down if asked.

Can you grab somebody's link list and use it on your site? Not if there is any creativity in how it was devised or is arranged or displayed. The legal answer is that a random list—or one that is simply an alphabetical listing, like a phone book—is not copyrightable, but if it looks as though some real time or effort went into the list, don't steal (all of it).

Can you create an internal frame and link through to other sites, displaying their content on your page? The legal answer is no. Context is everything on the Web, and if you are taking more than fair use allows, but less than the totality, you're in a (dark) gray legal area. Come back to the light. This is true especially if the other site has ads and you frame only content, surrounded by ads on your site.

5. The Scope of Your Copyright.

As a journalist, you care about your copyrights. In a world in which journalism is increasingly practiced by freelancers, stringers and others who don't get a single paycheck from a single employer, controlling your copyrights is crucial. Not surprisingly, publishers—whether in paper or on the Internet—want your copyrights. If you are hired to do a piece for a particular employer, your employer already has the copyright under the "work for hire" rules. If not, be careful what you sell. Time, space, geography, and medium can be specified in the copyright of a single article. (Although all big media outlets will make you sign away everything as part of the contract before you get paid.)

Note also that what you publish online—not only on your Web site but also to a listserv or Usenet group—doesn't lose its copyrighted status unless you sign it away. So if someone takes your material and reprints it elsewhere, speak up.

In the Digital Age you needn't cause or be the victim of any train wreck. In fact, there needn't be a train wreck at all. The existing rules will work well in protecting property rights and the rights of a free press. The efforts of governments, businesses and assorted zealots to change those rules radically on the grounds that media are changing radically are much more likely to result in a disaster.

As a journalist, you must be particularly on guard. You can no longer afford to think like a passenger—now you must begin thinking like an engineer.

James Wheaton is founder and senior counsel for the First Amendment Project, a public-interest law firm that protects peoples' First Amendment rights to learn about and participate in public affairs. He is also president of the Environmental Law Foundation, a public-interest environmental justice enforcement program in Oakland, California. He has taught media law at Stanford University and in the journalism department at San Francisco State and is the former executive director of California Common Cause. He is a graduate of Brown University and of the University of California at Berkeley (Boalt Hall).

chapter **10**

Issues in the Future of Journalism

The question of credibility on the Internet is the most precious—and hard to establish—commodity online.
—Leonard Sellers

Trying to look into the future is always filled with risk. New Age fortune-tellers talk about special ways to see into the crystal ball through "scenario planning," and other schemes, but the future cannot be seen clearly. By trying to plot curves from the past and see dim outlines ahead, however, journalists are granted one great opportunity: to begin preparing.

Students of journalism seek facts, whether those facts uphold their hopes or not. Journalists approach facts with healthy skepticism, but welcome all viewpoints. Before we send you on your way into the future, let's pause for a breath and wonder for a minute what awaits you.

Quite bluntly, there will be no future if Leonard Sellers' warning about credibility is not understood and heeded. A great deal of time is devoted to *how* to create animated GIFs, *whether* **3-D imaging** will burst data pipelines and *why* **vector imaging** is superior to alternatives using **bitmaps.** For those deeply involved in online authoring and Web development and for all code warriors this mindset is excellent. There is no minimizing the importance of skills needed for the production of good storytelling. But that's just half the story. More than that, it is the other half of the story. Let's start with a simple question: What are the goals of journalists? Before embarking on their great journey into the future, journalists, must pause to consider not only where they are going but why they are going there. Here are some proposed answers:

- Journalists are going where the technology will allow them to go, to destinations not reachable before. In their ongoing voyage they will have the ability to tell important stories of scope, depth and force previously unimagined.
- Journalists are going there because it is their responsibility as students of journalism to set the high mark, to raise their standard and to define the state of the art.
- Journalists are going there because media are the central circuit board of modern human societies. They are concerned that if they do not go there, people who are irresponsible, greedy and antisocial will dominate those circuits, endangering everyone.

The next generation of journalists will welcome this journey, knowing that with power comes accountability. They are not zealots, refusing to see the dangers of their assumptions, but journalists, seeking out the dangers and criticisms ahead.

Doubts About Online Journalism

Perhaps the most common concern raised by thoughtful critics is the worry that the Internet will allow, indeed, will fuel, divisions among different economic classes, age groups, ethnic backgrounds and genders. Their reasoning goes something like this: Why would members of one of these groups go to an online news site that does not solely represent a viewpoint usually associated with them? Why would people go to a news site that tells them what they stand for is untenable?

In a world of mass media, whether people are listening to NPR's "All Things Considered," watching CNN's "Headline News," or reading the national edition of the Los Angeles Times, they will be exposed both to stories they find inspiring and to stories they find unpleasant. And although even total media saturation will not expose the audience to all the elements of life's rich pageant, any mass media exposure will convey the message that the world is a very big place, with many competing aims, and that it is bigger than any individual.

That message reinforces the opportunities for journalism to survive and prosper. Let us consider the World Wide Web. It is, in fact, not a web at all, but a set of very independent cells linked only by wires and radio waves. It represents a mass medium of the future that looks something like cable TV, with, instead of 500 channels, 500,000 or even 5 million channels. How will journalists find a way to use this capacity? Will they have the time to spend at Web sites that are unreliable and that dispense information with little real value to achieving their goals and perhaps even with the destructive effect of stopping their success?

Imagine that you are looking for information about the presidential impeachment process. If the sites you visit are dominated by extreme left or right wing material, are you getting the full picture? More important, what will the lack of good information mean to the audience? Smart decisions—decisions that lead to survival and prosperity in a political, academic, business or social environment—are made only when people are armed with full information, not with partial information or with misinformation.

In the long term the World Wide Web may prove to be the greatest factor in history in bringing people together. Why? The huge amount of news and information available on the Web of today and tomorrow compels people to consider much more diverse information. People go to the Web because they need to, and journalists with greater access to more of this data will be the best equipped to survive and prosper.

Already at this early stage of Web development, however, threats to the survival of journalism are evident. Perhaps the most visible symbol is a fellow named Matt Drudge, who isn't really a reporter but plays one on the Internet. He has the props (a Walter Winchell hat) that serve as a recognizable trademark, helping to move product. He has the boring and hard-to-use Web site implying that he is a serious person and not a frilly, bells-and-whistles New Age media man. He has a steady stream of gossip that, like fortune-telling, gets something right once in a while—to much acclaim. But he also gets so much wrong so often that he does a disservice to everyone—journalists and nonjournalists alike. Not that Matt Drudge and the so-called new media newspeople who are like him are demons, but they do represent a counterpoint to the kind of true quality journalism that must win in the long term.

The consequences of these destructive elements suddenly grown from the Web were evident in an early debacle involving former newspaperman, network news correspondent and presidential spokesman Pierre Salinger. He announced to the world that he had discovered that the sudden explosion of TWA Flight 800 off the coast of Long Island, New York, in July 1996, was caused by a U.S. military missile. His announcement, because of his standing, was covered widely. When real reporters asked him to attribute his statement, he said he had read it on the Internet.

The sites Salinger used were run by nonjournalists who had little or no concern about accuracy, multiple sourcing, independent verification, libel or fairness. The result of Salinger's initial pronouncement and subsequent insistence resulted in a sad ending to a long and distinguished career.

There are more prosaic arguments against getting involved with online journalism. Although thousands of newspapers around the world have created online sites and are hiring scores of young journalists at above-average salaries to run them, how many will become and stay profitable, after strong early starts remains an open and controversial question. When the economy goes sour again, as it most certainly will in the cyclical capitalist rhythm, will those people be the first to go? And just how much real journalism will they get to do, as opposed to sitting in front of a tube and writing code all day?

Good questions, and questions *you* will have to answer as you take control and chart the future course.

Opportunities for Doing It Right

If there is no challenge ahead, why bother? Challenge fuels the best of us. If coasting on someone else's achievements is your way of work, work somewhere else. Journalism is simply not for you.

Once committed to the fundamentals of good reporting, editing and producing, journalists can look to some of the major challenges currently facing the area of online journalism. Perhaps the most argued question in news organizations that run both traditional and new media (a newspaper or broadcast news operation and an online site, for example) is whether to post breaking news on the Web before publishing or broadcasting it. On the one hand, the news organization wants to take advantage of the incredible speed of the Internet and be the one to break the story. On the other hand, the organization doesn't want to beat its own primary news vehicle and tell competitors what it has. Then again, the organization wants to use the Web site as a promotion for its primary news product (or, in new media lingo, *core product*). But it doesn't want to make it unnecessary for people to purchase the newspaper or to watch or listen to a broadcast because they saw the story on the Web already.

Although these issues were discussed in some depth in Chapter 3, it is appropriate to mention again here that one of the great strengths—and caution points—of the Web is speed. The around-the-clock **news cycle** created by the Internet is helping push the news industry forward, and, points out Dave Kansas, editor in chief of TheStreet.com, "it presents a very different challenge. Working on the Internet requires a bold combination of accuracy, quality and timeliness."

Experienced journalists know that extraordinary time pressures translate into extraordinary risks for making mistakes. Thoughtful online reporters, editors and producers will have to deal with this paradox decisively. There are no simple, template answers. The answers depend on your site, your other news products and your readers, viewers and listeners. The model of The Wall Street Journal (http://www.wsj.com), which charges for use of its Web site, does not work for the Arizona Republic (http://www.azcentral.com), which does not charge.

The Wall Street Journal is the only mass media newspaper that successfully charges customers to read it in online. This practice allows it greater freedom in breaking stories, although serious competitors no doubt read the online version regularly to be sure the Journal is not scooping them. The Arizona Republic is a regional, not a national, paper and has fewer competitors, allowing different kinds of opportunities.

Some surveys, though, have found that as many as half the people logging onto online newspaper sites are from outside that publication's traditional circulation area. One reason for this finding may be the widespread use of search engines that point people to sites regardless of geographic location when those people are looking for information about broad topics, such as medicine, or about specific topics that might come under the beats discussed in Chapter 3. People may also visit nonlocal sites when they are looking for travel information about regions. Research compiled by the Newspaper Association of America identifies significant opportunities for online newspapers in locations that attract large numbers of visitors. After all, who better to tell tourists where to stay, eat and entertain themselves than the best-informed business in town?

Organizations such as the Newspaper Association of America are involved with a growing amount of research on Internet journalism as mainstream corporate backers increasingly create and acquire online presence. The research often debunks myths that may hold back the Web journalist.

Reprinted with the permission of the Newspaper Association of America.

Once more, the basic question you must ask is what are your goals for an online news site and how are they best achieved, knowing there will be trade-offs and compromises. Each **market** is different.

Just as newspapers expanded beyond simple political and commercial news with the creation of the popular press more than 150 years ago, online news sites are quickly realizing they have the potential to offer more than just hard-core, breaking news. Among the possibilities are entertainment guides, interactive programs to provide travel directions, the latest airline fare deals. Original thinking is rewarded most richly in an original environment, and the Web is that.

In addition, it will not be enough simply to rehash print and broadcast stories online. Every online news site must develop original news stories created for its medium or the audience will have little reason to go to the Web for news and information. Although these enterprises may be started slowly, journalists must take that first step lest they wake up to find that nonjournalists are so far ahead they'll have to work twice as hard to catch up.

The future for sites that take advantage of true multimedia is bright. Think you can do TV news better than what you see on the air today? The Web will one day let you put your money and time where your mouth is. What about radio? Both? A large camp in the online news and information business argues that old brand names for established news outlets are not good to use for a Web presence. Ronald Dupont Jr. of the St. Petersburg *Times* says he's "glad to see many papers are no longer pushing their newspaper names as their URL but, rather, are going to regional names." Dupont says his site is a good case in point. For three years the paper had been promoting http://www.sptimes.com. Then "we switched to http://www.tampabay.com." The number of visitors to the site jumped "at least 50 percent across the board."

The Sarnoff company, named after the NBC pioneer, offers an example of how one television enterprise is looking to use the Web. In conjunction with several partners, Sarnoff is working on plans that would allow traditional TV stations and networks to beam Internet data in high-definition digital signals directly to a computer or similar device at a person's home or work or on the road.

The same thing is happening in commercial radio as well. A growing number of radio outlets are already involved in setting up radio broadcasts over and through the Internet. They stream directly into the home, office—and perhaps most important from a commercial sense—automobile and other portable Internet devices. This means that very soon, people interested in news (or sports programs or any other subject) of a very specific nature will probably be able to listen to almost anything they can dream of.

■ The Work Ahead

There are about 70,000 new users of the Web every day, with a grand total soon to reach 100 million people. And in 1998 we learned of a major evolution in Web use: 20 percent of people online were going online exclusively to access news.

There is much to discover in the years ahead. Before full broadcast bandwidth becomes widely available, journalists must move away from the

19th century's reliance on words to communicate and take the first baby steps toward a full use of multimedia to tell stories. Bigger screens, higher resolutions and faster speeds are already here, clearly pointing to the future direction of news and information.

The tools of Web authoring will also change dramatically in the next several years. For now, serious students of journalism should be acquainted with the basic tools of online authoring, such as HTML, Photoshop and audio software. Programs such as BBEdit allow Web authors to create with their own custom coding, but take care of some of the heavy slogging.

Many people are already using what people in the industry call WYSI-WYGs, pronounced "WIZ-ee-wigs," and short for "what you see is what you get." These Web page editing programs, such as HomeSite or NetObjects Fusion, have different levels of complexity. Some are so easy that school-children in the first grade are using them to build Web pages. Some are complex and challenging enough that professional Web developers use them for their work. The more complex the program, the more opportunities it offers authors to break out of simple templates and let their storytelling imaginations rip.

The time will almost certainly come in online journalism, as it has in the 50-year-old-plus broadcast industry, when the technical production side will be separate from the reporting side. The two specialties will work together on the news product, and some knowledge of the basic components—the material addressed in this book—will be absolutely necessary. For journalists who want to realize their vision of the future and who want to be in a position to influence the major direction online journalism will take, a strong understanding of both sides of the production enterprise will be crucial.

Online journalism is very much an ongoing venture, and you can never say, "Okay, I've learned enough." The real challenge is to paddle furiously to the right place before being swept away by the current.

▉ A Parting Salutation

"Who is a journalist?" was asked in the preface to this book. "Anyone who recognizes and protects the sanctity of what we do, who subscribes unswervingly to an ethical canon grounded in balance, fairness, restraint and service," answers Ted Gup of Georgetown University. "Published online or in print, it matters not."

The work of the creators of online journalism begins with imagining—imagining not only their work, but also the future and their role in it. Like the creation of all things, the creation of this medium will take hard thought, serious time and discipline. It will probably take some money. These are things you must provide yourself.

What this book offers is a broad map outlining the hard-won knowledge gathered over years of labor. The online site will continue to provide depth and scope regarding journalistic issues and techniques—a virtual university library of help for brainstorming, precision coding and, most important, quality journalism guidance.

It is not the aim of this book to turn the best and brightest students of journalism into computer coders, desk drones and format followers. Its aim is to couple the solid and sharp skills of true journalism to the power of an online world where the buzz phrase "Information Age" has wide and deep meaning. Those students with the imagination, the hard work and the intelligence to break out of the template news sites now online will one day be known as the true parents of the next great breakthrough of journalism. They will be not merely the journalists of this new century, but the creators and managers and owners of journalism into the next generation and beyond.

"The Web is transforming culture, it is transforming language, transforming information, and we're seeing this in very dramatic and measurable ways," says media critic Jon Katz. "All the rules are being rewritten. It is unlike anything we have seen before."

This book's mission is to help create and sustain real reporters, editors, producers and publishers for this new age, carrying an ancient torch still burning bright after a long and tumultuous journey. The trust, sacrifice and dedication that brought journalism to this point were too hard fought to leave behind now, when journalism stands on the threshold of its greatest challenge—and its greatest triumph.

Farewell to the Web

JOHN MARKOFF

There was a period of more than a decade, from perhaps 1978 to 1994, when as a reporter I was a true believer in the power of the Net.

As a struggling freelance writer in the Silicon Valley I discovered the ARPANET and became a quick convert. For many years it offered me a window into technology subcultures that few people had access to. I wrote stories both about the potential of computer networks to transform society and also about the dark side of the Net—about computer crime and computer outlaws.

Electronic mail also offered an avenue for gaining access to company engineers and executives that few other reporters had. Moreover, the idea of electronic network communities held tremendous allure. In the mid-1980s I was one of the first participants on the Well, the quirky Sausalito, California, conferencing system that was a forerunner of the online chat phenomenon that was to follow.

Then, with the rise of the World Wide Web, everything changed. Commercialization led to explosive growth. Overnight, the insular Internet community of engineers, academics and scientists became a vast cybernetic shopping mall. At the same time newspapers began responding to the real threat to their revenue base by creating online editions.

Web publications, both exclusively online and the Internet versions of traditional print and electronic media, have since proliferated. In the space of a half decade online journalism has become a tremendous force in the world. News from anyplace in the world is available everywhere instantly. The Net is a great democratizing force—you no longer need to own a press or work for someone who does to be a reporter.

It sounds utopian; however, I'm no longer a convert. Increasingly I've found myself a skeptic, moving away from the Web as a reporter.

The reason is simple. So far—and I emphasize the "so far"—for all the overnight millionaires the Internet has created, online journalism has not led to any dramatic increase in the quality of reporting.

Indeed, I have this recurring nightmare: Online journalism succeeds only well enough to completely undercut the existing financial underpinnings of print journalism. It progressively steals both circulation and classified ad revenue, thereby crippling newspapers already under siege for demographic and other reasons. In their place online publications fail to erect any grand new institutions committed to the journalistic enterprise.

The result is a vast morass of Matt Drudges, data-mined infomercials and unending streams of tiny newsbytes regurgitated by an all-encompassing set of Web portals. It is a dystopian world described first in the TV series "Max Headroom."

Look around. It seems like my nightmare is coming true. Why, I want to know, has the Internet not produced an I. F. Stone? On the surface it is the perfect medium for such a brand of committed independent journalism. But if a young I. F. Stone is out there I haven't found him. Instead we have an infinite number of Matt Drudge wanna-bes intent on the titillating quick hit and quick buck.

Is there a way out?

The one reason that I'm not a total cynic today is the fundamental driving force underlying all of this, Moore's law: Every 18 months the number of transistors you can put on a silicon chip doubles. Moore's law led to the rise of the personal computer and the Internet, and one thing that is certain is that the industrial process that unleashed all this chaos on the journalistic world is not slowing down—it's accelerating.

This means that the technology we are just beginning to grapple with today will be entirely transformed tomorrow. For example, the Internet has touched about half the U.S. population and far less of the rest of the world, yet the rapid dispersion of digital wireless networks and mobile Web browsers is certain to make the Net more ubiquitous than either the telephone or the television in a few short years.

How will that change journalism? Nothing will be stable. Nothing will be permanent. Just as the Internet snuck up on the world in the last decade, things will continue to be transformed in ways we can't conceive of today.

And maybe my nightmare won't come true. Maybe the advent of inexpensive, portable, flat-panel displays will lead to a flowering of interactive journalism.

After all, the French Revolution went through its own journalistic crisis in a struggle over authorship and anonymity. Maybe from this digital revolution a new set of journalistic standards will emerge.

I hope so.

John Markoff is a senior writer for the New York Times. Based in San Francisco, he covers the Silicon Valley, computers and information technologies. Before coming to the Times in 1988 he covered the Silicon Valley for the San Francisco Examiner beginning in 1985. He has also been a writer at Infoworld and in 1984 he was West Coast technical editor for Byte Magazine. He is the co-author with Katie Hafner of "Cyberpunk: Outlaws and Hackers on the Computer Frontier" (1991) and with Lenny Siegel of the "The High Cost of High Tech" (1985). In January 1996 Hyperion published "Takedown: The Pursuit and Capture of America's Most Wanted Computer Outlaw," which he co-authored with Tsutomu Shimomura. He was named one of Upside Magazine's Digital Elite 100 in 1996, 1997 and 1998.

Glossary

33.6K

A common transmission speed used by many modems. Refers to the speed of transmission between a computer and Web server. Once known as *baud* rates, the common measurement has now been replaced by the more accurate BPS, or bits per second. The bigger the number, the faster the speed. A 33.6K modem transmits data at 33,600 bits per second—a typical, and relatively slow, speed.

3-D imaging

Refers to images on a screen that appear to be in three dimensions. This can be achieved through using voxels (a volume pixel—a unit of graphic information that defines a point in three-dimensional space, compared with a regular pixel, which is a 2-D space) or through a sophisticated coding language such as Virtual Reality Markup Language (VRML).

56K

The fastest speed a standard telephone line can transmit data through a standard modem.

actualities

The term used in radio to describe audio such as sound bites, natural or wild sound and other special sound elements in a story.

analog

The way information is normally, naturally and traditionally recorded. For example, in this printed glossary the words are recorded one after another. In analog videotapes (most movie videos for home use are analog) images are recorded sequentially one after another. The counterpart is digital, or nonlinear, recording, which uses a numeric code to store and retrieve information.

animated GIFs

An animated GIF is a graphic image on a Web page that moves. GIF stands for graphics interchange format.

ASCII

Pronounced "ASK-ee." A program for writing text that is not a word processor, in other words, does not have a spell or grammar check or other fancy editing functions, but is a stripped down program used in applications such as WordPad and SimpleText. ASCII stands for American Standard Code for Information Interchange and is the most common format for text files in computers and on the Internet.

audio information

Information picked up through our ears. For example, if we hear the sound of leaves rustling, we immediately think it is windy or there is something in the leaves causing them to move against each other. Audio information, like visual information, is a natural and powerful way to communicate without words.

bandwidth

The pipeline size of digital data going to and from computers on the Internet. Full bandwidth allows real-time video, like the video seen on television. Since most of today's bandwidths are smaller (a smaller pipe), trying to stuff all the data needed by a large video file is incredibly slow.

BBS

Bulletin board service. See **bulletin board.**

betacam

The current, but quickly becoming outdated, camera most professional television news and programming photographers use. Beta is generally analog and provides an excellent picture, but it is being replaced by digital cameras for reasons of economics and quality.

bites

Also known as sound bites. The sound recordings of what print journalists call quotes.

bitmap

A bitmap defines the space and color for each pixel, or bit, on a Web page. GIFs and JPEGs use bitmaps. Bitmaps use a fixed or raster method of specifying an image, compared to a vector graphic image, which can be resized with more ease. Often, a Web author makes an image using vector graphics and then saves it as a raster graphic file or bitmap.

bookmark

In the popular Netscape browser, bookmarking is a way to mark, keep and retrieve designated Web sites. The same function is performed in the equally popular Internet Explorer browser through Favorites.

breaker

Generally used as a shorthand in newsrooms for a breaking story.

breaking event

A story that is happening and changing quickly as it is being covered, and requires on the spot, fast-changing reporting.

breaking news

Another popular shorthand term for a breaker and breaking event.

B-Roll

In television news, the videotape shown while the reporter or anchor is narrating off camera. Also often referred to as VO or voice-over tape.

browser

The software program used to view the World Wide Web, such as Netscape, Internet Explorer or AOL (American Online, which now owns Netscape), among others.

bulletin board

A place on the Internet where people can post an opinion, a message or anything else, much like a real bulletin board in a Laundromat or student union. Also known as a BBS, or bulletin board service. The term is being replaced by *chat room* or *message board.*

bundled

Usually refers to products that are put together in one marketable package. For example, Microsoft bundles most of its big business applications such as Word, Excel and Power Point into one bundled product sold together, called the Office Suite.

cascading style sheets

A relatively sophisticated tool, generally not for an introduction to Web design. Cascading style sheets, or CSS, dictate what order or precedence the style, or appearance, will take when there are conflicts within different browsers. The main point of CSS is to provide more control over the appearance of a Web page for the page creator rather than for the audience.

chatroom

See **bulletin board.**

click art

A commercial term for what is more commonly known as *clip art,* referring to artwork that is not owned and is available to anyone. Also sometimes referred to as canned art.

click-through rate

A click-through is a commercially vital measurement of how many people click on an ad on a Web page, which generally takes them away from that site to the site of the advertiser. The click-through rate is the percentage of ad views (the ad simply appears on the page where the audience can see it) that resulted in click-throughs. A click-through rate of 0.15 to 1 percent is considered good; 5 percent is excellent. Because a click-through is highly desirable for the advertiser (if not for the site with the ad), the click-through rate serves as a prime factor in the price paid by the advertiser to the site that displays the ad.

clip art

Traditionally used in print journalism to get images (or art) that are not owned by anyone in particular and are in the public domain.

commercial service provider

A term usually associated with services such as America Online that allow full Internet access after going through their site, which is a portal to the Net. The distinction between a commercial service provider and an Internet service provider is fading.

compressed video

A means of removing some of the frames from a video clip, making it slimmer and able to move through the Internet at faster speeds.

compression

A way to remove either video frames or sound frames from a file.

copy block

In print, especially newspapers, usually a paragraph of information accompanying and explaining a photo or other illustration. It is substantially longer than a *cutline,* or caption.

cover

In television news, covering means using pictures that cover sound bites. A cover is usually used to break up the visual monotony of a long bite. For example, if a firefighter is talking at some length about the flames burning down a building, some or all of the sound bite could be covered with pictures of the flames.

cursor

The blinking icon on a computer screen that shows where the person is typing.

cutline

An abbreviated version of the copy block, one or two sentences at most. Also known as a caption.

DHTML

Dynamic HTML promises to allow high-level Web authors more freedom to create pages that are more animated and more responsive to audience interaction than are those created with previous versions of HTML. Possibilities include having the color of a text heading change when the user passes the mouse over it or allowing the user to drag and drop an image to another place on a Web page. DHTML also promises to enable cascading style sheets.

dissolve

A method of changing pictures in film and television in which one element fades into the next. A current favorite is a *digital dissolve,* in which little geometric shapes of the picture break up and dissolve to another picture. Other methods of changing pictures include a sharp *cut* from one element to the other and a *wipe* from one to the next (which can look like turning a page or wiping the scene from one end of the screen to the other).

download time

The length of time it takes for information to download from the Web server to the audience's computer.

downloading

When information goes from a Web or file server into a personal computer.

DSL

A digital subscriber line is a faster-than-average way to bring high-bandwidth information to computers over ordinary telephone lines. DSL allows transmission rates of up to 6.1 megabits (millions of bits) per second, enabling continuous transmission of motion video, audio, and even 3-D effects.

e-mail

The most used portion of the Internet, e-mail is the ubiquitous software that allows people to send messages across the Internet from one computer to the next. It is not part of the World Wide Web, which is a different part of the Internet.

embedded images

Pictures, graphics and other illustrations seen on a Web page.

evergreen

An old news term for stories that are good for long periods of time and not necessarily dependent on a fresh news hook. Evergreen stories are also sometimes derisively referred to as *chestnuts.*

file

A term used here to refer to a single document that contains a specific set of data. The file is generally available to use in a personal computer, on a file or Web server or on another network of computers. The file must have a unique name that allows another computer to find it and access it. For example, this glossary is in a file titled, cleverly enough, "Glossary." A picture or other graphic embedded in the file would have its own unique name, such as glossary.gif, allowing the computer getting into that file (i.e., accessing it) to understand that it is a GIF.

file sizes

File size is crucial on the Web. Relatively slim file sizes (10 kilobytes) can go through the Net quickly and download quickly. Big file sizes (anything over 50K) will take longer to squeeze through narrow bandwidths and download.

flaming

Slang for insulting people in e-mail. For example, after someone posts a question on a Listserv, someone might denigrate that inquiry as being stupid or ill informed. This rude, vulgar and ignorant behavior is called flaming.

folos

A traditional news term for following a news story. For example, when a crime story that has attracted attention goes from a police action to a court action, a good news organization will folo the latest newsworthy developments.

frames

Most Web sites today have frames. They are the separate Web pages visible together within a site, typically, a navigation bar on the left side (that serves as an index or table of contents), a page to the right that is the page the person clicked on in the navigation bar, and another frame or two for advertising or some other part of the site. Each frame is controlled independently.

FTP

File Transfer Protocol. The computer protocol used to move a file from place to place, usually from one computer to another over the Internet. Its cousin is HTTP, or Hypertext Transfer Protocol, which is the way most files are transferred on the Web portion of the Internet (hence the URL that starts http://www . . .). Another cousin is SMTP, or Simple Mail Transfer Protocol, which transfers e-mail.

gigabyte
One billion bytes, a very large amount of space on most computers.

graphical
Refers to the graphic, or nontext visual information element, on the Web.

hard drive
The main memory for a computer.

hard news
News that is pegged to a current or breaking event, such as a crime story, election or disaster, and is told in a matter-of-fact manner.

home page
The main page, document or screen of a Web site.

HTML
Hypertext Markup Language, the basic computer protocol for moving files around on the Web. A subset of Standard Generalized Markup Language (SGML).

hyperlinks
The formal and slightly old-fashioned way to refer to links on the Web. Links allow the audience to click from one Web page or site to another.

hypertext markup language
See **HTML.**

Internet
The vast network of computers that began communicating with each other through dedicated lines in 1969. It was first known as ARPANET.

Internet Service Provider
Also known as ISPs, these are the most commonly used service for getting on the Internet.

inverted pyramid

A traditional news format for telling a story, especially in print. The idea is to sum up the most important and interesting aspects of the story at the top (the lead) and then start explaining details below, ending with the least important and least interesting aspects.

ISP

See **Internet Service Provider.**

jump cut

In video editing, a forbidden way to cut pictures. A jump cut would typically be used in a street scene, for example, making it appear to be one continuous shot when it is actually two separate shots, one immediately after the other without clear definition. In a jump cut, there is a lack of continuity, so that a person might be standing or walking in one place and then be suddenly gone or somewhere else.

links

See **hyperlinks.**

mailing lists

Electronic mailing lists that typically use software programs such as Listserv. People using e-mail on the Internet can read and write messages on these lists. People who subscribe to a mailing list receive e-mail from everyone who subscribes to the list, and in turn, their messages are sent to everyone else to read.

market

A broadcast term for what demographers call Standard Metropolitan Statistical Areas, or large metropolitan regions. The top five of the 200 defined broadcast markets in the United States are New York City, Los Angeles, Chicago, Philadelphia and the San Francisco Bay Area.

megabyte

One million bytes of data. Also see **Gigabyte.**

message board

See **bulletin board.**

MHz

The abbreviation for megahertz, a measurement of speed in electricity. In computers often referred to as *clock speed*.

modem

The device that commonly connects a personal computer with the Internet, usually through telephone lines.

monitor

Any cathode-ray tube (CRT) screen used to watch TV, the Internet or video.

mouse

The device used by most computer users to move the cursor.

mouseover

A colloquial way to refer to interactive images. In a typical mouseover the person uses the mouse to move the cursor onto an image; a graphical element then appears, providing more information, such as another link, picture or text.

MP3

A popular means to move audio across the Web. MP3 is an abbreviation for MPEG-1 Audio Layer-3. It compresses audio into a very small file (about one-twelfth the size of the original file) that retains the original level of sound quality when played.

multiple sourcing

The vital journalistic technique of getting information from more than one source. Stories that do not have multiple sources are often derisively called *single-source stories.*

natural sound

Often referred to as *nat sound,* the audio used in a story that is not someone talking to the reporter, but is naturally *in* the story, such as a passing train blowing its whistle or a police officer yelling at a suspect to lie down. The reporter stops narrating (or *traking*) the story and brings the nat sound up.

Net

Shorthand for the Internet.

network

In information-technology terms, a series of points or nodes interconnected by communication paths. Networks can interconnect with other networks and contain subnetworks.

news cycle

In traditional media, the morning and the afternoon newspapers have defined the news cycle. In broadcast, which uses the term less, it refers to the morning, evening and late-night news shows. The term also refers to the daily rhythms of the news. For example, an astute public relations person will release a good story to maximize the news cycle, knowing that Saturday morning has the lowest circulation and Sunday morning has the highest for a newspaper.

news feature

Unlike a hard news story, a news feature is usually less time-dependent, can take longer to report, write and produce, and remains interesting to the audience for longer period of time.

news hole

A print term referring to the amount of space left for news after the ads are placed.

news hook

The actual event that makes the story new and consequently newsworthy. For example, a story about the danger of drugs might be hooked to someone well-known who is dying from a drug overdose.

newsgroup

A gathering of people on the Internet who participate in a written discussion of a defined subject. The e-mail is collected at a central Internet site and redistributed through Usenet, a worldwide network of news discussion groups on the Net. Some newsgroups are moderated by a designated person who decides which postings to allow or to remove.

NITF

Short for News Industry Text Format, a standard Web code proposed for news pages online. NITF would be a single, commercially supportable, straightforward method for coding, exchanging, and archiving news stories. The same NITF-coded files could be used for print, the Web, broadcast and archives. NITF uses XML tags.

nonlinear

Usually refers to a digital format. Unlike an analog recording, a nonlinear recording is not stored or retrieved in a special order or sequence. It is stored with numeric codes, allowing users to pull up what they want instantly, without having to run through everything recorded before the desired item.

nut graph

A print news term that refers to the heart of the story. In a hard news story it is usually the lead. In a news feature story is it usually in the first three to five paragraphs. It is often also called the "so-what" graph. In English classes, it might be referred to as the "topic sentence."

operating system

The system that runs a computer; the essential backbone software program. Personal computers, such as those manufactured by IBM, Dell or Gateway, usually use Windows by Microsoft. Apple Computers use the Mac operating system. Other systems used include Linux.

page jump

In print, where the story stops because of space and jumps to another page, where it is continued and usually completed. Most readers do not read past the jump (especially if the *nut graph* is past the jump).

page views

A common term that refers to a person's opening up a Web page. It is one measure used to set advertising rates on the Web: the more page views, the higher the cost of advertising. Also see **click-through rate.**

peripheral

Any device attached to the main computer, such as a printer, modem or zip drive.

pixel

Short for picture element, a pixel is the essential building block of everything seen on a computer screen. All the words, graphics and other elements on the screen comprise hundreds of thousands of these tiny points of light, which are made of varying intensities of red, green and blue.

plug-in

Plug-ins are computer applications installed as software accessories to the browser. Among popular plug-ins are Adobe's Acrobat, RealNetworks' RealAudio, and Macromedia's Flash. There are hundreds of plug-ins available, some free, some not.

port

A port is a socket or receptacle usually found in the back of a computer. Ports come in many shapes and sizes, but all serve one purpose—to enable information to get in and out of the computer directly. Some of the most familiar ports are SCSI (pronounced "scuzzy"), serial and MIDI.

porting

Americans have an unalienable right to turn nouns into verbs, and the verb *porting* (derived from the noun *port*) can mean something as loose as sending data from one computer to the other. However, it usually refers to connecting different machines, especially peripherals such as storage devices, to computers.

post

Put something on the Web.

pro bono

The Latin *pro bono publico,* commonly shortened to pro bono, means "for the public good." It is the common term used by lawyers for donating their services.

processing speed

See **MHz.**

processor

A set of electronic circuits that can perform a computation. The word is commonly interchangeable with CPU, or central processing unit, the actual computer.

public domain

Intellectual property not owned by anything or anyone.

RAM

Random access memory. The memory, or storage, immediately available to the computer and computer user. Storing something in RAM is like keeping it on top of the desk, well within reach. When the computer is asked to fetch or create a document, it can do so relatively quickly because the document is in RAM—nearby. Something stored on the hard drive, in memory or storage, is like the material stored in a desk drawer or filing cabinet: it takes a few more steps to get to.

real-time audio

Audio files that sound exactly as they did when recorded. They may be compressed in a popular program such as MP3, but play back in real-time.

real-time video

Video shot at 30 frames a second.

refreshed

A computer renews the screen 50 to 75 times per second—in technical terms, that's a refresh rate. In Web jargon refresh has taken on the meaning of updating a page. Because a breaking story can change quickly, online journalists must constantly monitor and refresh stories that have been posted.

router

On the Internet, a device that determines how data will be sent to its destination. A router can be located at any juncture of a network.

saved to disk

The process by which one saves work on a computer. Once it is saved to disk (the hard drive or a floppy disk), it is legally protected as copyrighted material.

scalable

Able to be increased or decreased without the user's having to buy a new computer.

scoop

When a reporter is the first to *break* a story and has it exclusively (at least for some period of time). Sometimes called a *beat*.

scroll

The arrows on the sides of the browser that allow the user to move the screen up and down and sometimes back and forth.

site

Web site.

sound files

Computer files that contain audio information.

sound under

A broadcast term used to describe sound that is lowered and kept under a dominant sound. For example, a broadcast news reporter or anchor may read a story about a train while under the voice the audience can hear the *natural* sound of a locomotive going by.

sound up

Like *sound under*, but the natural sound becomes the dominant audio factor. For example, to punctuate a piece about a train, the broadcast reporter or anchor might pause in the narration and bring up the sound of the locomotive passing by with a shrill whistle.

source code

The raw HTML code that works behind the glossy interface seen by the audience. Web audiences are able to see the source code behind Web pages by pulling it down the menu at the top of the browser. For example, while visiting a Web page using Netscape Navigator, you can go to the pulldown menu View at the top of the frame (or "chrome") and select Page Source to see the HTML tags.

spider

A computer program that goes to Web sites to read their pages and other information in order to create entries for a search engine index. The major search engines on the Web all have such a program, also known as a *crawler* or a *bot.*

spray

A broadcast term for taking lots of relatively casual video of a scene, usually panning from one side to the other, up and down, and focusing from a wide shot to a narrow, detailed picture. A producer might tell a photographer, "Just spray the place."

stand-up

In television news, a stand-up is when the reporter is seen on camera, sometimes with a microphone. Stand-ups should be used only for necessary transition points—segues—or as a *close* to the story. ("This is so-and-so reporting for the 6 o'clock news.")

stick microphone

The microphone used by broadcast reporters that usually has the station's name or logo (*bug*) on it. More sophisticated news operations tend to use small microphones attached to a coat lapel to reduce the barriers between the reporter and the audience.

stream

Streaming is a way to send video or audio in compressed form over the Internet so that it is displayed or heard by the audience as it arrives. In this way, the audience does not have to wait to download a large file before seeing the video or hearing the sound. A player, a special program that uncompresses and sends video data to the display and audio data to speakers, is needed for streaming. Major streaming technologies include RealSystem G2 from RealNetworks and Microsoft Windows Media Technologies, such as NetShow.

switches

In telecommunications, a switch acts very much like a router but is generally a simpler device. Switches select a path or circuit for sending data on to the next destination.

T-1

One of the faster alternatives to the slow modems that most Web users still have. Transmission rates hover around 1.544 MBPS. Another level, the T-3 line, allows 44.736 MBPS and is also commonly used by ISPs. The T-carrier system is entirely digital.

tables

Tables are useful ways to display information and lay out Web pages. Standard tables look something like this:

Each cell contains information.

tags

The letters and symbols typed in a document that translate into what looks like a Web page when viewed through a browser.

thumbsucker

An old-fashioned newspaper term for a story that takes a long time to read, often a long feature piece in the Sunday paper.

uploading

Putting something on the Internet.

URL

Uniform Resource Locator. The Web address, such as http://www.NewsPort.sfsu.edu.

Usenet

The portion of the Internet where newsgroups live.

vector imaging

Refers to vector graphics, which is a set of mathematical formulas that describe the shape of each image. Vector imaging ensures that graphics will appear on the audience's screen at a high resolution. Raster or bitmapped graphics do not always have the best resolution levels.

visual information

Information taken in visually. An enormous amount of information can be absorbed at a glance, although print technology leads to the almost unquestioned belief that information must be written.

VRML

Virtual Reality Markup Language. An early subset of HTML that allows 3-D images to be used on the Web. Pronounced VER-mel.

web server

A program that serves the files that form Web pages to the Web audience.

WebTV

A box sold by many manufacturers, usually set on top of a TV, that, with the appropriate software and modem, allows the audience to view and use the World Wide Web on a television.

wide shots

A photo term for a shot taken from far back, allowing a large, if somewhat distant, picture. Usually used to set a scene.

wild sound

See **natural sound.**

window

The area on the computer screen where the person is looking at the Web. A person can view more than one site on the World Wide Web at a time by keeping one site open and starting another browser window.

World Wide Web

The portion of the Internet invented by Tim-Berners Lee in 1989 and first posted in 1990; it is the second most popular aspect of the Net after e-mail.

XML

Stands for eXtensible Markup Language, a Web-authoring code that provides a flexible and standard language for Web pages. For example, two different news sites might use XML to list the attributes of automobiles. The audience would then be able to compare all the cars on the same basis, even if the Web sites were completely different. Many people say that XML and HTML will be used together in many Web applications.

Index

Los Angeles | London | New Delhi
Singapore | Washington DC

SAGE Publications Ltd
1 Oliver's Yard
55 City Road
London EC1Y 1SP

SAGE Publications Inc.
2455 Teller Road
Thousand Oaks, California 91320

SAGE Publications India Pvt Ltd
B 1/I 1 Mohan Cooperative Industrial Area
Mathura Road
New Delhi 110 044

SAGE Publications Asia-Pacific Pte Ltd
3 Church Street
#10-04 Samsung Hub
Singapore 049483

© Ray Pawson 2013

First published 2013

Apart from any fair dealing for the purposes of research or
private study, or criticism or review, as permitted under the
Copyright, Designs and Patents Act, 1988, this publication
may be reproduced, stored or transmitted in any form, or
by any means, only with the prior permission in writing of
the publishers, or in the case of reprographic reproduction,
in accordance with the terms of licences issued by
the Copyright Licensing Agency. Enquiries concerning
reproduction outside those terms should be sent to the
publishers.

Editor: Katie Metzler
Assistant editor: Anna Horvai
Production editor: Ian Antcliff
Copyeditor: Jennifer Hinchliffe
Proofreader: Jill Birch
Marketing manager: Ben Griffin-Sherwood
Cover design: Wendy Scott
Typeset by: C&M Digitals (P) Ltd, Chennai, India
Printed by: MPG Printgroup, UK

Library of Congress Control Number: 2012942929

British Library Cataloguing in Publication data

A catalogue record for this book is available from the British
Library

ISBN 978-1-4462-5242-0
ISBN 978-1-4462-5243-7 (pbk)

Library
University of Texas
at San Antonio

To Wendy

Contents

About the Author

Ego

Ray Pawson is Professor of Social Research Methodology in the School of Sociology and Social Policy, University of Leeds. His main interest, perforce, is in research methodology and he has written widely on the principles and practice of research, covering methods – qualitative and quantitative, pure and applied, contemporaneous and historical. Publications include *A Measure for Measures* (1989), *Realistic Evaluation* (1997) and *Evidence-Based Policy: A Realist Perspective* (2006). He was elected president of the Committee on Methodology of the International Sociological Association (1994–98). He has served much time in prison (for research purposes), being a former UK director of the International Forum for Education in Penal Systems (1995–97). He has held the post of visiting professor at the University of Rome, University of Victoria, Canada and the Royal Melbourne Institute of Technology, as well as visiting fellow at the UK Economic and Social Research Council's Centre for Evidence-Based Policy and Practice. He is best known for his writing on evaluation methodology, research synthesis and evidence-based policy, work which has been supported over the years by four ESRC senior fellowships. Research income exceeds £3.5 million. He has acted as researcher and consultant on programme evaluation for the various UK and European government departments and agencies.

Alter Ego

'God save you, dear reader, from an *idée fixe*, better a speck, a mote in the eye.'
Joaquim Maria Machado de Asiss – *The Posthumous Memoirs of Bras Cubas*

Ray Pawson's idée fixe, which goes by the name of *realist inquiry*, has travelled through thirty years and three previous books – one on measurement, one on evaluation research and one on research synthesis. And now here he is in 2013, with *The Science of Evaluation*, doggedly, stubbornly, unendingly writing manifestos in the name of realist social science. A number of institutions have supported this work and along the way he has been fortunate enough to receive several fellowships and visiting positions. He is world famous in Italy, Tasmania and Vancouver Island. Happily, the idée fixe remains controversial. Other bodies (unnamed for the purposes of this sketch) have not been so enamoured and social inquiry has fragmented into a thousand rival fragments. Undaunted, he is already working on a new book – *How to Think like a Social Scientist*.

I am some kind of realist, some kind of critical, hypothetical, corrigible, scientific realist. But I am against direct realism, naive realism and epistemological complacency.

Donald T. Campbell, *Methodology and Epistemology for the Social Sciences*, 1988

Preface: The Armchair Methodologist and the Jobbing Researcher

What enables and yet constrains research? What is both medium and outcome of research? What do researchers reproduce without even knowing it? What is supposed to unite researchers but may divide them? What empowers researchers to speak but is never fully articulated? What is played out in the routine of research but can never be routinised? What is the responsibility of all researchers but for which none has a mandate?

The answer to all of these riddles is METHODOLOGY. Methodology provides what has been variously described as the procedures, the rules, the codes and the laws of scientific research. But methodological procedures are unlike the exacting drills followed, say, by airline pilots in readying a plane for take-off. Methodological rules are unlike, for instance, those in official rulebooks enforced by referees and followed by sports teams for fear of the penalty. Methodological codes are unlike, for example, the highway code with its compendium of regulations and advice designed as behavioural conventions for all road users. Methodological laws are quite unlike the legislative decrees sanctioned by governments, written in statute and sustained by enforcement regimes.

Scientific methodology shares with these other regimes the ambition to clarify and organise. But the crucial difference is the extent to which the procedures, rules, codes and laws are formalised. In all of our other cases, there is a manual to follow or a handbook to be thumbed or a rulebook to be consulted or an authoritative tome to be pondered. To be sure this guiding documentation is often in a state of steady evolution, with even the two hundred and fifty-year-old Marylebone Cricket Club, the driest and dustiest of regulatory bodies, responding with continued clarifications and amendments to the rules of that game. The crucial point in these other cases is that vested authority is marshalled via a codified set of decrees and propositions.

Consider, by contrast, the rules of the scientific game. Each time the researcher dreams up a project, responds to a tender, enters the field, draws conclusions, makes observations and pens a paper, that individual too will work under a set of expectations. Indeed many researchers consider that they operate under the sternest of requirements – that of producing scientific truths about the fragment of the world selected for study. But whether they are peering down a microscope or into the human psyche, whether they are smashing atoms or counting heads, they do not begin the day by consulting the manual. They have no rulebooks to which to refer, no regulators to affirm standards and no sanctions to keep them honest.

There are methodological rules, of course, but they are soft centred and mutually applied. They exist within the institutional norms and tacit knowledge of the research community. There is no executive body. There is no hard and fast division between legislator and legislatee. Self-scrutiny, peer review and organised distrust provide the levers of control. If science was merely a matter of routine and compunction, of compliance and rule following, it would be pre-programmed – done already or awaiting completion in the pipeline. In reality, scientific research undergoes constant change as fresh discoveries are made and new fields open up. Accordingly, methodological rules cannot be carved in stone. They must allow for creativity and indeed they must innovate as the natural and social worlds change about us and so fashion novel investigative challenges. Methodological rules are therefore adaptive – principle informs practice but innovative practice may yield fruit and gradually embed back into the principles. Each time the researcher dreams up a project, responds to a tender, enters the field, draws conclusions, makes observations and pens a paper, that individual will seed minute modifications to the methodological rules.

I begin this book with this brief soliloquy on methodology as a solemn memorandum to myself of the challenges to come – for I am about to pontificate on the procedures, rules, codes and laws of a little corner of scientific inquiry known as evaluation research. I am about to write a book on methodology – and not for the first time. How does this work? Or, to put it more combatively – if the rules of science are adaptive and collegial who vested you, dear author, with the authority to codify and formalise them?

I think it works like this. The wellspring of methodology is the repetition of certain procedures from investigation to investigation. Let us take as an example the most commonplace of social science methods, the interview. An author might take part in many interviews across many studies and thus reflect on instances that had been more successful and less successful. Further consultations follow with colleagues who have plied and pondered the same trade. The result may well be a textbook, which gathers together the rules of thumb and tricks of trade, so presenting what a group of investigators perceive as best practice. Recall that textbooks, for Kuhn (1962: 2), are crucial to the consolidation of scientific paradigms. Not only do they establish the philosophical footing and provide exemplars, they proselytise for a particular perspective.

Kuhn held a rather dim view of such monographs in the physical sciences, noting their tendency to convey a somewhat conservative, wrinkle-free, wrangle-free view of laboratory life. The same cannot be said of the social science 'methods' textbook. Some texts may be celebrated and regarded as authoritative. But the words of the armchair methodologist only remain definitive as long as the jobbing researcher continues to operate on the same foundations. The principles are sustained in practice. Given the untold complexity of society and the potentially limitless ways of studying it, there are always reasons why that practice may not be sustained. To return to our illustration, an interview may try to tap anything from mundane, face-sheet variables to the subject's innermost thoughts, so leading to the enormous, present-day portfolio of available methods (Gubrium et al., 2012). Jobbing interviewers may thus pick and choose. The result is that social science methodology is rather febrile. In Kuhnian terms, it is 'pre-paradigmatic' – unable to settle on a definitive set of first principles. Given the huge terrain of social inquiry, it is hardly surprising that there is a multitude of theories and methods. It is hardly surprising that some of these come and go. As anecdotal evidence of the fickle fate of methodological strictures in the field of interviewing, I note a marooned attempt of one scholar to persuade the world of the merits of the 'realist interview' (Pawson, 1996 – Google Scholar citation count 34). Before its time, no doubt!

It would appear, then, that there is something of a 'methodology market' in the social sciences and this brings us back to the issue of what it is that licenses methodological authority. What is it that generates the staying power of a particular approach? Occasionally, this is attempted by institutional closure. The methodological armchair becomes a throne. A group declares itself to be the executive and attempts to lay down the law on a particular sphere of operations. For an example here we come closer to home and consider the modus operandi of groups such as the Cochrane and Campbell Collaborations (www.cochrane.org/; www.campbell-collaboration.org/). Having devised what they consider a 'gold standard' approach to a particular form of research, namely systematic review, they then lay down the procedural rules. Hierarchies of evidence must be observed, protocols must be followed and study designs must be approved. If all of this is in place, then an inquiry is authorised and authenticated. Follow this formula and you will find yourself with an accredited, trade-marked publication.

Thankfully, in the febrile, pre-paradigmatic world of social science inquiry, researchers are mostly independent and not so regimented; they still pick and choose their methodology. The guiding and appropriate impulse is to tailor the method according to the perceived requirements topic under study. In other words, methodologies are sustained under the choices and preferences of those jobbing researchers designing the next inquiry and the next and the next. What is more, each inquiry will require a gentle adaptation of the strategy to meet the peculiarities of each situation studied. Methods gain their spurs by thoughtful adaptation rather than mindless replication. Methods come and go but some are more adaptable and thus sustainable. The underlying dynamic of the methodological market, it would seem, is one of the 'survival of the fruitful'.

And this is where I find myself. This book is about the stamina and staying power of the realist approach to evaluation research. Nick Tilley and I published *Realistic Evaluation* in 1997, following a good five years of forethought and deliberation. That book was about methodological choice, for at that time we considered the programme evaluation market rather limited: outcome driven, quasi-experimental approaches imported from clinical trials, processual studies uncovering the formative minutiae of local programmes, mixed in with a bit of constructivist tomfoolery. We proselytised for an alternative, focused on explanation and based on research designs which extracted, tested and refined programme theory. Other key authors shared and championed that mission (Henry et al., 1998; Mark et al., 2000). Other researchers began to share the labour and the terminology, analysing findings by 'context', 'mechanism' and 'outcome'. And even the policy community began to pay heed to the realist slogans, commissioning research to discover 'what works for whom in what contexts?'.

The strategy was further expanded in 2006, with the publication *of Evidence-based Policy: A Realist Perspective*. This book was prompted by the observation that evaluative studies have become industrial in proportion and by the thought, still very much with me, that even more power can be brought to the realist elbow and to the policy table, by extracting, testing and refining programme theories via existing evidence culled from the evaluation factory. And with this step 'realist synthesis' was born. The explanatory principles remain the same but with a different technical application – realist reinterpretations of all the operational stages of a systematic review were provided: establishing the review question, searching for primary studies, assessing their quality, extracting the data, synthesising the evidence, disseminating the findings, and so on.

The present text is intended to be a sequel to these two volumes. One can gain a crude measure of the staying power of ideas through citation counts and it is true to say that it would have knocked the socks off Pawson and Tilley in 1997 and Pawson in 2006 had they an inkling of the weight of present-day bibliographic references to *Realistic Evaluation* and *Evidence-Based Policy* (Google Scholar citations at the time of writing being 2668 and 488 respectively). But all of that is history and the aim of *The Science of Evaluation* is to progress, refine and extend key realist themes throughout applied social inquiry. To do so I have had to ponder on exactly what it is that leads to the survival of the methodologically fruitful. In this spirit, I have in mind four simple motifs to guide the development of the method and with which to infuse this book: i) practice what you preach; ii) share ownership; iii) stimulate debate; iv) address the most difficult challenges.

The first developmental strategy is easy to describe and, given sufficient time, the easiest to put into use. Since empirical practice is both medium and outcome of methodological principle, it is always important to combine the two in explaining the realist perspective. It is important for the armchair philosopher to become the jobbing researcher. Methodological wisdom, perforce, has been aided and abetted on each occasion that I have dreamt up a project, responded to a tender, entered the field, made observations, drawn conclusions and penned a paper. In the final chapter of the book I present a version of the latest, the most extended, and (I like to think) the best crafted of my attempts at realist synthesis (Pawson et al., 2011a). Previous publications on this research have concentrated on the specific policy implications, namely – is there evidence to support the effectiveness of a potential ban on smoking in cars carrying children? Here, the research is reported in two different ways: i) as an exemplification of all the practical steps and decisions that have to be made in conducting a realist synthesis, and ii) as a study of the limits to knowledge that emerge and always emerge from research synthesis.

This second developmental strategy, opening the method to collective ownership, happens, if it happens, under its own steam. At the time of writing there are over a hundred published studies utilising realist evaluation and more than a score of realist syntheses. It is these empirical investigations, rather than any methodological commentary, which embody the sustainability of the strategy. These evaluations and syntheses are located right across the policy waterfront – development studies, social care, urban regeneration, public health, crime reduction, agricultural extension, information science, wildfire prevention and so on. Accordingly, inquiries cover a bewildering array of 'whats' that may work, 'whoms' who may benefit and 'circumstances' that might respond to intervention. As each inquiry progresses, there will be a fresh challenge, one that the researcher deems untouched by previous investigations and unremarked in the existing texts and guidelines. Other researchers will confront similar challenges and collectively they, too, expect a piece of the methodological action.

One example of this, current at the time of writing (Greenhalgh et al., 2011), is the project: *Realist and meta-narrative evidence synthesis – evolving standards* (RAMESES). The aim is to spread ownership of these newer methods of systematic review by having a Delphi Panel, currently numbering 28 individuals with experience in realist synthesis, brainstorming, submitting personal views, exchanging theoretical and empirical papers, and using a simple voting system in order to try to establish some publication standards for these approaches. Whilst I cannot trace all of these developments between the covers of this book, Rameses can expect to leave his fingerprints. In short, there is a club out there of which this is an invitation to join.

The third development strategy, encouraging debate, sounds unremarkable but is truly a cornerstone of the scientific method. As each new realist inquiry progresses there is some resonance and some dissonance with the principles set down in the foundational texts, for as we have seen, real researchers do not simply rehearse scripts or follow recipes. Inevitably, it is the dissonance that is of interest and all the more so when the departure from the method constitutes a challenge to the method. Not all users of a method become wedded to a method. It is under such challenges, or under the scrutiny of what Campbell (1988: 513) calls 'the disputatious community of truth seekers', that methodological progress emerges.

Accordingly, in the second chapter of the book I examine some of the dispute that has gathered in the minds of would-be users of realist evaluation. As a preview, let me mention my favourite migraine-inducing issue – 'I can perceive endless b***** mechanisms and contexts in my programme but I cannot tell one from the other'. In short, some researchers have found it impossible to practise what I preach. My aim in this respect is to engage in conceptual clarification, to refine the exposition of some key realist concepts in order to make them more user-friendly. However, I should make it clear that the medium of clarification here is hard-headed debate. I respond to what I perceive as errors in the application of the method. Readers may be experiencing a whiff of contradiction here and would be correct in thinking that this hardly sounds like 'sharing control' of the method. Because the methodological debate will take place within the covers of this book, won't I load the debate? But sharing control of a method is not the same as ceding control. Methodological debates are there to be won and lost and they should be battled out in the open. To this end Chapter 2 is subtitled 'A Realist Diagnostic Workshop'. It is intended as a platform for further debate that, thanks to the brave new world of online communication, can be continued elsewhere. Here then is another invitation providing a right to reply, an opportunity to add further challenges, and a chance to enlarge the debate. This is all organised under a Sage website called *Methodspace*, which can be accessed at www.methodspace.com.

The fourth strategy for methodological development is to expose a strategy to its most difficult challenges. And where might realism stick out its chin? One methodological challenge dominates this book. It is the feature that generates headaches, triggers migraines and beckons frontal lobotomies for all hard-pressed evaluators and not just realists. I refer, of course, to the problem of complexity. It is the task of Chapter 3 to unravel the different layers of complexity confronting the evaluator but let us foreshadow the mission by noting that programmes are complex by dint of their multiple ambitions and multiple stakeholders, and on account of their long, adaptive and disputed implementation chains, and because the problems they seek to resolve are often interconnected, long-standing and deep-seated, and by reason of the diverse rules, customs, histories in the institutions and contexts in which they operate. And so on!

Now, how has realism fared in the face of complexity? Realist evaluation has many virtues but a mixed blessing is that it adds to the complexity of evaluation research. *Realistic Evaluation* encouraged researchers to dive into the black box and search out what it is about programmes that makes them work. So, to return to a favourite example, readers were urged to understand that CCTV cameras were only dumb, unthinking bits of glass, metal and electronics stuck on the side of buildings, which actually worked to reduce crime through the reasoning of the criminals, operators, ground staff, police and passers-by who encountered them. In this simplest of interventions a flurry of real explanatory mechanisms was thus identified – immediate arrest of those caught in the act, improved detection of those caught on camera, better deployment of police and security staff, increasing perceived risk for would-be offenders, promoting natural surveillance by creating safer environments, reducing the time for crime and so on (Pawson and Tilley, 1997b: 78). Complexity blossoms.

Another realist invective – apply contextual thinking – also increases the complexity of evaluative inquiry, and abundantly so. Realism urges evaluators to consider that all of the characteristics of all participants plus all of its institutional, cultural and historical surroundings were part of the programme. All might be decisive in its success. Previously, programme evaluation had a tendency to treat these factors as either confounding variables to be controlled out of outcome calculations or as immutable, pre-existing features that were not part of the implementation process under scrutiny. The contextual penny has now dropped. All evaluators now understand that what works in Wigan on a wet Wednesday will not necessarily work in Thurso on a thunderous Thursday. The problem, of course, is that contextual conditions are infinite and hardly limited to the British towns, climatic conditions, and weekly rhythms in this little jingle. Complexity snowballs.

The second book, *Evidence-Based Policy*, represents a move from single to multiple inquiries. The conduct of an evidence review, by its very nature, forces researchers into a headlong confrontation with complexity. Synthesis spreads inquiry, inevitably and inexorably, along the implementation chain and across the contextual landscape. One discovers that although a family of programmes carries the same name and harbours the same ambitions, it will never be implemented in the same way twice. For instance, in reviewing the effectiveness of Megan's Law in the USA (under the law the identity of a released sex offender is made known to the community in which he settles), the book examined the manifold decisions required in enacting the legislation (Pawson, 2006a, chapter 5). Which released sex offenders constitute a risk? When, where and how should the local community be notified of their presence? How can community response be channelled and controlled? How and to what extent should probation and police practices change? It soon becomes clear that there is little common ground in the way such decisions are made from state to state, and from county to county, and indeed from official to official. Complexity skyrockets.

In short, it can be said that the realist perspective, having called for an opening up of the 'black box' of interventions, now needs a way of replacing the lid. The entire second part of the book is devoted to that task. The way ahead is marked by an admixture of ambition and caution. Evaluation science needs to be more venturesome in widening the focus of inquiries from that of 'the programme' and should begin to consider 'policy ideas and their history' as its subject matter. It needs to avoid the perpetual, regressive habit of 'starting from scratch' and should expect each new investigation to respond to and develop from 'what is already known'. At the same time it is necessary to make absolutely clear that the terminus of evaluation research is, always and perforce, partial knowledge. Accordingly, the central task in all that follows is to defend and indeed to celebrate the never-ending pursuit of unobtainable truth.

Under the challenge of such a fine motto, I now offer a speedy rehearsal of the thesis to come. It is produced in three parts, which I like to think of as prequel, midquel and sequel. I am pretty sure, *Star Wars* apart, that there is no such word as 'midquel' but the idea is to suggest sequence in the argument and growth in the storyline. Part One looks back to the foundations of realist evaluation. Part Two wrestles with the present day challenges and with that tenacious opponent going by the name of complexity. Part Three contemplates the future and a wider, cinemascopic role for evaluation science. Each chapter has been designed to be read independently and so takes the bother to explain itself at the outset.

Part One. We begin in prehistory, before evaluation research had been weaned, with a brief chapter on the emergence and the present-day relevance of key realist ideas in philosophy and social science. Next is a chapter dealing with the methodological headaches left behind by the previous ministrations of Drs Pawson and Tilley. Hearty debate is joined as I seek to refine the basic conceptual apparatus of realism via a critique of the misadventures of other researchers who have found their own ways of conducting 'realist' evaluations.

Part Two. Complexity takes its bow in Chapter 3, with a concerted attempt to articulate its every nook and cranny as seen from a realist perspective. Given that the issue of complexity tops the agenda in all schools of evaluation and social science, Chapter 4 compares notes and seeks out the strengths and weaknesses of the rival 'solutions'. This is followed by the pivotal chapter of the book, an attempt to rewrite the principles of evaluation science under the challenge of complexity. I venture to suggest that evaluation research should significantly enlarge its explanatory ambitions, whilst acknowledging that its findings and policy recommendations will always remain partial.

Part Three. Chapter 6 is the first of three seeking to pursue some grander challenges of the now widened realist manifesto. It produces a programme theory for the much coveted ambition of 'behavioural change'. Revealed is the wave after wave of 'invisible mechanisms' that must be fired in shifting wavering, havering programme subjects and a sharp contrast is drawn with the naive pronouncements of the 'nudge' theorists. Clinical interventions, at large and as a whole, are the target of Chapter 6 under the argument that they are every bit as complex as social interventions. It follows that evidence-based medicine would benefit from a healthy dose of realism. Finally we come to the denouement of the tale, the circumambulatory Chapter 8, which attempts to practise in the space of a single investigation, all of the earlier preaching on the science of evaluation.

A brief conclusion contemplates dialogue with the chattering classes. It asks – how will the complex and partial truths of realist inquiry fare amidst the political clamour? A mixed picture emerges personified by two characters – the Steady Eddy of Realism and the villainous One-armed Scientist.

With the content described, I am now ready to commence my self-appointed task of refining the principle and practice of evaluation science. As I've tried to explain, methodological progress is a process that no one superintends. Methodologists do their thinking rather noisily – out loud, in texts, on the rostrum and the soap box. For jobbing researchers methodological decisions are muted and ceaseless and made in confronting the *next* fieldwork problem. Both ways are true ways and I have tried to infuse and balance the book with work on both the principles and practice of realist inquiry. For a methodology to advance, its philosophers and practitioners, its arm-chair dwellers and field-workers, and its farmers and cowmen should be friends.

Speaking of which, it is a pleasure to introduce and thank the many colleagues who have roamed the realist prairies with me and who, according to the cunning alibi I have concocted above, share co-responsibility for all the blunders and pratfalls that I am about to make. Geoff Wong, Lesley Owen, Sanjeev Sridharan, Trish Greenhalgh, Gill Westhorp, Joanne Greenhalgh and Ana Manzano have joined me in several recent projects and publications and their ideas, their labours, and some of their words are imprinted onto the following pages. Mark Monaghan, Jenny Hewison, Nick Emmel, Frans Leeuw, Nicoletta Stame, Elliot Stern, Mike Kelly, Kieran Walshe, Rob Anderson, Mark Pearson, Alex Clarke, Patricia Rogers, Greg Ogrinc, Paul Batalden, Don Berwick, Dave Byrne, Malcolm Williams, and Martyn Hammersley have all proved valuable allies in a variety of intriguing sub-plots. Last and hardly least, thanks to Nick Tilley for joining me in that initial, insightful stroll in Meanwood Park. One must never omit the vital institutional support and I hereby acknowledge awards from two UK bodies, the ESRC (Economic and Social Research Council) and NIHR HS&DR (The National Institute of Health Research: Health Service and Delivery Research programme). Thanks also to Katie Metzler and Anna Horvai, the new team at Sage. Much better than the old bloke. My unedited texts can be a pain and I am grateful for the painstaking work of Ian Antcliff, Jennifer Hinchliffe and Jill Birch, the production team at SAGE for bashing it into shape. For further proof that one can judge a book by its cover, grazie ancora a David dalla Venezia. With apologies from my forgetful brain to anyone omitted from a now lengthy list of sympathisers, there is one final lexicographical task before we enter the labyrinth.

'Realism' – What's in a Name?

Once again, I've produced a book marching proudly under the banner of 'realism'. It has become increasingly problematic to do so because as realist inquiry has flourished it has also divided. It is useful, therefore, to attempt to clear up a little terminological confusion at the outset. Donald Campbell (1988: 444) found himself in a similar difficulty some three decades ago in an utterance I have used as the epigraph for this book: 'I am some kind of realist, some kind of critical, hypothetical, corrigible, scientific realist. But I am against direct realism, naive realism and epistemological complacency.' It would take a chapter or two to sort through this little lot of realisms, so I will settle for noting that Campbell's (1988) critical realism is not the same as Bhaskar's (1979) critical realism: the former being about promoting criticism and counter criticism in the community of scientists; the latter being about the possession of a privileged, normative standpoint with which to criticise other interpretations of the world. Campbell's other realisms are based on a view that science is a perpetual process of theory testing, thus always beginning in the 'hypothetical' and still ending in the 'corrigible'.

My own usage of realist terminology has also wobbled in wordage if not in meaning. The strategy developed here was first termed 'scientific realist' analysis (Pawson and Tilley, 1997a). We used the phrase because the mantle of science has been grabbed, wrongly in our opinion, by these favouring experimental trials. We also favoured it because the method was identified squarely with a generative view of causation which had come to the fore in the philosophy of science.

A couple of years later Tilley and I dropped the prefix 'scientific' and settled on the phase 'realistic evaluation', though this was intended as a title of a book rather than the name for the method. We still insisted on pursuing the high scientific objectives of objectivity and generative causal explanation but also wanted to emphasise that evaluation research had a different cause from other social sciences, namely to have realistic ambitions to inform real-world policy and practice.

Thereafter, the simpler phrase 'realist evaluation' became the norm, partly because it was also the preferred nomenclature of other authors (Henry et al., 1998; Mark et al., 2000). I continued in this usage when I enlarged the approach to cover systematic review methodology, which in realist guise, for obvious reasons, became 'realist synthesis'. In other outlets I have referred to 'middle-range realism' (Pawson, 2000) in order to stress membership of the theory-driven school of evaluation research and usage of an explanatory formula following closely upon Merton's middle-range theory.

In the present text, I had a sneaking ambition to return to my original term, 'scientific realism', based on continuing solidarity with and the further development of Mertonian and Campbellian methods. As this would only have seeded further confusion I have decided to stick, and proudly so, to the terms 'realist evaluation' and 'realist synthesis'. Though to mark some broadening ambitions I also introduce the term 'evaluation science' in an attempt to decouple evaluation research from its moorings in the analysis of single interventions. Evaluation science has ambitions to shape the widest domains of policy inquiry and is served by the methods of realist evaluation and realist synthesis.

In the spirit of Campbell I close this lexicon by noting that I, too, am 'some kind of realist'.

PART 1

Precursors and Principles

The aim of Part One is to establish the book's realist foundation and, to the best of my ability, create a level playing field for all readers. Realism, as a form of scientific explanation, has a long history. Realist evaluation and realist synthesis are new kids on the block. They should be understood as workaday research strategies that have done their utmost to embody the principle of realist explanation. They are attempts to remain faithful to key tenets from the philosophical page and to apply them in the practical struggle to make sense of the policy mêlée.

Chapter 1 establishes some key realist principles, the seven pillars of realist wisdom no less. I've chosen to do this with some economy by selecting seven key authors and highlighting their particular contributions. Drawing up the shortlist was something of a headache. Lavish excuses are made to those not making the cut. The point to note is that the realist endowment belongs to the philosophy of science, the sociology of science and to social science methodology more generally. Only two jobbing evaluators are encountered and, even here, discussion revolves around their Herculean ideas on evaluation's guiding principles. The Pillars of Hercules appear on the cover page of Sir Frances Bacon's *Novum Organum* (1620), with the inscription, 'Many will pass through and knowledge will be the greater.' I like to think the same applies to anyone encountering the foundations established here.

Chapter 2 pays close attention to the founding concepts of realist evaluation. As with any other method, realist inquiry develops its own terminology. Realist evaluation centres around exploring the 'mechanisms', 'contexts' and 'outcomes' associated with an intervention. For any would-be users of the method, questions immediately erupt – what are these things, how do I spot them, how many of them need to be dealt with, how should I understand their balance? Although, I have striven to make all of these matters clear, it is inevitable that in other hands these core ideas will be reshaped. The purpose of the chapter is to thus further refine the key apparatus of realist evaluation by engaging in debate with other realist evaluators and other realist inquiries. As explained in the preface, the whole point is to collectivise ownership of the strategy.

Chapter 1 represents work done in the realist armchair. Chapter 2 transfers realism to the field. The aim of Part One is to make them equally comfortable environments.